T0309927

Comprehensive Judgment
and Absolute Selfessness

Comprehensive Judgment and Absolute Selfessness

Winston Churchill
on Politics as Friendship

John von Heyking

ST. AUGUSTINE'S PRESS
South Bend, Indiana

Manufactured in the United States of America.

1 2 3 4 5 6   24 23 22 21 20 19 18

Library of Congress Control Number: 2018931423

The paper used in this publication meets the minimum requirements
of the American National Standard for Information Sciences - Perma-
nence of Paper for Printed Materials, ANSI Z39.48-1984.

St. Augustine's Press
www.staugustine.net

Table of Contents

Preface

Histories and biographies of Churchill make frequent mention of his friends. Some comment on their importance but few bring their importance into focus. Indeed, he rarely spoke of his friendships. However, his concern for friends and for friendship always seems to hover above, or in the background, of his statecraft and in his thinking about statecraft and politics. This book brings that background into focus by showing how friendship plays a central role in his moral vision of politics and of what statesmanship consists.

Regarding friendship as a key to politics seems archaic or even elitist today in the minds of many. But for many of the greatest statesmen of the past and even of contemporary times, friendship has been the central category of their statecraft and their moral vision of politics.

Churchill was one of those statesmen. This book examines friendship as the core of Churchill's moral vision of politics by considering both his practice of friendship, as well as his thoughts on friendship in political life. It examines some of the friendships he conducted in his political life, including with Lord Birkenhead (F. E. Smith), Lord Beaverbrook (Max Aitken), and Franklin D. Roosevelt. It also examines his historical and political writings to explain how he regarded friendship also as a goal for political life. He regarded Parliament as a club of friends who esteemed their friendships, as parliamentarians who are custodians of the common good, as nobler than the partisan differences that divided them. The idea of trans-partisan friendships also animated the "Other Club" he founded with Birkenhead. Indeed, Churchill thought parliamentary democracy especially depends upon the friendliness of its statesmen and its citizens in order to mitigate the heat of factional strife. For him, parliamentary democracy in particular depends on personal friendships of the highest order to sustain the forms and formalities of the regime, as well as the political friendship upon which they are based.

His biography of his great ancestor John Churchill, the Duke of Marlborough, is his greatest statement of his political wisdom. It consists also of a sustained statement on the centrality of friendship in politics. His view of Great Britain as an "island story" is also his expression of a political friendship expressed as a long historical adventure, much as he regarded his personal friendships within politics as great adventures. Because adventures get sung about, he was its main singer, whose "songs" appeared as his speeches and extensive historical writings.

As a book about Churchill's moral vision for politics, this book asks a philosophical question by considering his life, political actions, and writings. This book is not a biographical or historical description of Churchill and his friends. It draws upon the work of the historians and biographers that offer a rich collection of empirical materials that invite investigation into the political purposes and moral vision that animated Churchill. This is more of a character sketch, or a work of "empirical political philosophy" because of the philosophical exposition it provides of the actions and speeches of a creative prince such as Churchill. It describes how Churchill understood friendship as the essence of statesmanship.

This book is an attempt to understand the role friendship plays in politics from the perspective of one of its greatest practitioners. The idea of writing came when I was writing a previous book, *The Form of Politics: Aristotle and Plato on Friendship*, which considers the question from the perspectives of the two great ancient Greek philosophers. I had to ask: do their philosophical ideas reflect political practice? To answer this question, one must look not to petty and average politicians but instead to great statesmen who exhibit greater thoughtfulness toward their craft. The present book answers that question in the affirmative. While Churchill read Plato's and Aristotle's political writings, his having done so matters little to my argument. Practicing politics in terms they would recognize, but unconsciously or without intending to, actually strengthens their case, and my case too.

This book would not have been possible without the gift of friendship I have shared with those involved in political life and who understand the central role friendship plays in their vocation. I have also enjoyed the gift of friendship with my fellow adventurers in "empirical political philosophy." My thanks go to: Richard Avramenko, Ken Boessenkool, David Goa, Grant Havers, Thomas Heilke, Collin May, Dallas Miller, Marco Navarro-Genie, Tilo Schabert, and Travis D. Smith. I thank Daniel Mahoney for his careful reading of the manuscript and helpful suggestions. Merle Christe provided crucial editorial assistance, and Sonya ensured my prose made some sense. Errors and omissions are due to me alone.

I also thank Bruce Fingerhut for his friendship and for taking the risk in publishing this book.

With the hope the study of political philosophy and the actions of statesmen can show the dignity of politics, friendship, and the common life citizens can enjoy together, this book is dedicated to my children: Geoff, Evie, Audrey, and Sebastian.

Part One
Politics and Friendship

Chapter One
Churchill's Political Vision of Friendship

What a fine thing it is to listen to such a bard
As we have here—the man sings like a god.
The crown of life, I'd say. There's nothing better
Than when deep joy holds sway throughout the realm
And banqueters up and down the palace sit in ranks,
Enthralled to hear the bard, and before them all, the tables
Heaped with bread and meats, and drawing wine from a mixing-bowl
The steward makes his rounds and keeps the winecups flowing.
This, to my mind, is the best that life can offer.[1]

Why Friendship is Important for Politics

Aristotle makes the following startling claim in his famous discussion of friendship:

> [F]riendship seems to hold cities together, and lawmakers seem to take it more seriously than justice, for like-mindedness (*homonoia*) seems to be something similar to friendship, and they aim at this most of all and banish faction most of all for being hostile to it. And when people are friends there is no need of justice, but when they are just there is still need of friendship, and among things that are just, what inclines toward friendship seems to be most just of all. And friendship is not only necessary but also beautiful, for we praise those who love their friends, and an abundance of friends seems to

---

1   Homer, *Odyssey*, IX.1–12.

be one of the beautiful things. Moreover, people believe that it is the same people who are good men and friends.[2]

Aristotle's glowing praise of friendship, especially its importance for politics, is difficult for us to appreciate in our day. Schooled in modern social science, with its roots in Machiavelli and his teaching that friends are mere instruments for the prince's power, we are more likely to view Aristotle's claim as naïve or quaint, typical wishful thinking of the philosopher who lacks the experience in the grit of actual practice in politics. Or perhaps his claim serves simply as window-dressing for cronyism or oligarchy. Thus we find it easy to understand the irony of the term, "Washington friend," which is to say that we recognize there are no genuine friends in politics. We are more inclined to understand political order as bound by procedures and rules to restrain the strong, to preserve rights and obligations, and to regard friendship as at best supportive of legal right, but more likely corrosive of it because friends tend to prefer their own instead of abiding by the universal legal order that obliges all.[3]

But it is our view of politics, and of friendship—not that of Aristotle—that is simplistic. Ask nearly any practicing politician whether his friends are important and of course he will respond in the affirmative. Indeed, friendship, along with its associated virtue of loyalty, could be seen as the *lingua franca* of practical politics, even among those who seem unable to achieve anything higher than a "Washington friendship." If a scientific approach to politics is to have any use at all, it must "maintain the phenomena," as Aristotle says.[4] Practicing politicians must be

---

2   Aristotle, *Nicomachean Ethics*, 1155a2231.
3   For a more sustained critique of such legalism and the social science upon which it is based, see John von Heyking and Thomas Heilke, "Introduction," *The Primacy of Persons in Politics: Empiricism and Political Philosophy*, xi.
4   "To speak, then, of friendship in the primary sense only is to do violence to the phenomena, and makes one assert paradoxes; but it is impossible for all friendships to come under one definition. The only alternative left is that in a sense there is only one friendship, the primary; but in a sense all kinds are friendship, not as possessing a common name accidentally with-

able to recognize their own activities in the scientific accounts of their activities, and the relative inability of scholars and the reading public to articulate the place of friendship in politics is symptomatic of a wider intellectual malaise.

In *This Town*, Mark Leibovitch describes extensively a culture of "Washington friends"—social and political climbers in Washington, DC, who seem to practice the kind of friendship that Thomas Hobbes describes when he says "to have friends is power; for they are strengths united."[5] Unsurprisingly, these same individuals are extremely lonely and crave companionship, but their stunted intellectual and moral characters prevent them from understanding their own plight or even articulating it coherently. They resemble the shades of the dead whom Odysseus meets, who must drink human blood so they can speak.[6] Unfortunately for us, the shades in Hades are more articulate than the bloodless shades of today because they are unable to utter speech beyond partisan clichés. Their failure at friendship, both personal and political, prevents them from transcending faction, which Aristotle saw as the political aim of friendship.

It is the purpose of this book to bring to light the manner in which friendship is a central category for politics. There are various methods available to demonstrate this. One is to examine the ideas of major political philosophers on friendship.[7] Another method might be to consider the implicit aspirations of such "Washington friends" and other contemporary politicians, and to consider whether implied in their deformed friendship is a yearning for a complete form of friendship like the kind Aristotle had in mind when he discusses virtue-friendship. This approach

out being specially related to one another nor yet as falling under one species, but rather as in relation to one and the same thing" (*Eudemian Ethics*, 1236b21–26. For discussion, see Stephen Salkever, "Taking Friendship Seriously," 77n.10).

5   Hobbes, *Leviathan*, ch. X.

6   Homer, *Odyssey*, XI.25.

7   See my *The Form of Politics: Aristotle and Plato on Friendship*. A broader range of thinkers are treated in this collection of essays: *Friendship and Politics: Essays in Political Thought*, edited by John von Heyking and Richard Avramenko.

would be a difficult exercise, akin to discerning how the shadows on the wall of a cave correspond to the light of the sun outside of the cave.

This book takes a third approach, which is to consider the actions of one of the greatest statesmen of the twentieth century, Winston Churchill. Like anything else in life, one needs to look to the examples of an art's greatest practitioners to learn that art. In the case of politics, Churchill stands out within the last hundred years. Moreover, it is one thing to follow the logic of Aristotle's ideas, or even to wish they were applicable to political practice. It is quite another to see them worked out in the actions and self-understanding of a statesman of Churchill's stature.

Friendship was for Churchill a central category of his statecraft. In politics he sought the virtue-friendships that Aristotle describes of those who exercise the highest moral and intellectual character. As Andrew Roberts observes, Churchill rarely spoke of his friendships, and Kenneth Young points out that he was slow to make friends.[8] However, when he made friends they were very close friends who were pivotal for his political success. He befriended men including Lloyd George, F. E. Smith (Lord Birkenhead), Brendan Bracken, Max Aitken (Lord Beaverbrook), Jan Smuts, Harry Hopkins, and Franklin Delano Roosevelt.[9] "Virtue" may be an unlikely way to describe the characters of these individuals. Indeed, Churchill's wife, Clementine, disliked the three "B's" (Birkenhead, Bracken, and Beaverbrook) on account of the bad habits, including gambling and drinking, they brought out in him. Indeed, Clementine's biographer claims Beaverbrook "was for a long time her most loathed

---

8   Andrew Roberts, *Masters and Commanders*, 44; Kenneth Young, *Churchill and Beaverbrook*, 11.

9   The present study focuses on his friendships with Beaverbrook and Roosevelt as a way of illuminating his statesmanship. On his friendship with Lloyd George, see Robert Lloyd George, *David & Winston: How the Friendship Between Churchill and Lloyd George Changed the Course of History*; on F. E. Smith, see David Freeman, "The Friendship Between Churchill and F. E. Smith"; on Brendan Bracken, see Charles Lysagt, "Churchill's Faithful Chela," 43–45. Richard Steyn's *Churchill and Smuts: The Friendship* was published after this book went to press. See references in later chapters for Beaverbrook and Roosevelt.

personal enemy," though he later became "a devoted fan."[10] Beaverbrook also appears to have inspired Evelyn Waugh's vapid character, Rex Mottram.[11] What Churchill seemed to find attractive in friends and cronies was, in Roy Jenkins' description, their status as a "sophisticated outsider" and the "touch of loucheness" in their character.[12] These qualities, which Churchill himself shared to some degree, seemed to suggest for Churchill the types of character who could serve as allies with whom to fight political and military battles, but also as companions with whom to enjoy the greatest action and dramas that life has to offer. Indeed, Roosevelt sent a telegram to congratulate him for winning a vote of confidence in January 1942, telling him: "It is fun to be in the same decade with you."[13] Character played an important role for Churchill when it came to choosing his friends.

Friendship then is not simply instrumental for some higher political goal, it is the primary goal of politics. Or, in the words he provides to serve as the moral of his biography of John Churchill, the Duke of Marlborough: "One rule of conduct alone survives as a guide to men in their wanderings: fidelity to covenants, the honour of soldiers, and the hatred of causing human woe."[14] This has less to do with helping friends and harming enemies, than the more Socratic view of helping friends and not harming enemies, where harm means primarily moral harm. Churchill wished to destroy Hitler's capacity for evil; he did not wish his moral corruption to worsen.[15]

Statecraft is an adventure best practiced and even enjoyed with companions who share one's stature. Of course finding such friends is

---

10   Sonia Purnell, *Clementine: The Life of Mrs. Churchill*, 5. My study purposely omits discussion of his most important friendship, with Clementine, because of the enormous complexities involved in understanding the friendship that is marriage. Purnell's biography demonstrates its political significance. I thank Peter H. Russell for this reference.

11   George Weigel, "'A Tiny Bit of a Man': Evelyn Waugh's Anticipation of Donald Trump."

12   Jenkins, *Churchill: A Biography*, 648.

13   Winston Churchill, *The Second World War*, vol. 4, 62.

14   Winston Churchill, *Marlborough: His Life and Times*, vol. 2, 996.

15   Plato, *Republic*, 331d–332d.

difficult because friends of similar stature to Churchill were rare. Even so, his moral and political vision is one of great friends performing great deeds with one another, and also of reflecting upon those great deeds in the form of sharing stories over dinner and drink, conversations, writing books, and even philosophical contemplation. Moreover, Churchill conceived of Great Britain as enjoying a political friendship—*homonoia* or like-mindedness in Aristotle's terminology[16]—that he termed its "island story." Political friendship, as friendship generally, is not only expressed through stories, but *are* stories, which helps explain why the histories Churchill wrote were primarily moral histories, which he saw "as a branch of moral philosophy" and not academic or scientific histories.[17] The moral of the story was not simply the meaning of the actions described therein, it was also about its main character, the author. As he said on one occasion of his *The Second World War*, "This is not history, this is my case."[18] His histories, of which he is a self-narrator, was a matter of what the ancient Greeks called *logon didonai*, the giving of an account of one's self, of holding oneself responsible to another for what one thinks and does.

Churchill had read some of the writings of Plato and Aristotle as part of his self-education after Harrow in the 1890s, and in his *My Early Life* he mentions the idea of philosopher-kings in Plato's *Republic* as a "crystallization of much that I have for some time reluctantly believed".[19] F. E. Smith (Lord Birkenhead) once gave him a copy of the *Nicomachean Ethics*, "the greatest book" ever written. Churchill appreciated it but remarked that "it is extraordinary how much of it I had already thought out for myself."[20] Indeed, it matters little for my presentation of Churchill's practice of friendship in politics whether he had read a word of Aristotle, because the practice of politics itself points logically toward

16 Aristotle, Nicomachean Ethics, 1155a20–30; 1167a25–30.
17 See John Keegan, "Introduction," *The Second World War*, vol. 1, x. On political friendship as story-telling or myth, see my *Friendship is the Form of Politics*, chapters 3, 5–7, and Conclusion.
18 Jenkins, *Churchill: A Biography*, 824, citing Gilbert, *"Never Despair," 1945–1965*, volume 8 of *Winston S. Churchill*, 315.
19 Jonathan Rose, *The Literary Churchill*, 24, 29, citing *My Early Life*, 115.
20 F. E. Smith (Lord Birkenhead), *Contemporary Personalities*, 115.

friendship. Indeed, commenting on Churchill's response to Smith, Harry Jaffa remarks on this very point of Aristotle's practical political science: "But it is the very genius of Aristotle—as it is of every great teacher— to make you think he is uncovering your own thought in his."[21] Coming at the problem of politics and friendship from the other, theoretical and philosophical side, it is in the study of Churchill's practice that one can gain genuine insight into Plato and Aristotle's insights. In a 1946 letter to Karl Löwith, Leo Strauss makes a similar point when he explains that he could not understand what Aristotle meant by magnanimity until he saw the example of Churchill.[22] So too we can understand the idea of political friendship in the practice of Churchill's statecraft. Thus does practice inform theory, and theory inform practice.

Festal Friendship Above Politics

In 1911, Winston Churchill (then a Liberal), with his good friend, F. E. Smith (Lord Birkenhead), formed the "Other Club," a dining club that included notables of British society for the purpose of convivium. The two were best of friends but they were also rivals, especially over the issue of Home Rule for Ireland. Frequently in ill health, Smith died at age 58 in 1930 and Churchill would never again have such a deep friendship (though I consider two close "seconds," Lord Beaverbrook and Franklin Roosevelt, in later chapters of this work). The "Other Club" was so named apparently because the two had been rejected by "The Club" that had originally been founded by Samuel Johnson and Joshua Reynolds, and whose current members included Herbert Henry Asquith and Arthur Balfour.[23]

But the "Other Club" was more than simply a club for Churchill's friends and cronies. John Colville explains that the greatest criterion for membership was the number one rule for any kind of companionship with Churchill: men with whom it was agreeable to dine.[24] One must be

---

21 Harry Jaffa, "Aristotle and the Higher Good."
22 Letter to Löwith, August 20, 1946, 111.
23 Chris Wrigley, *Winston Churchill: A Biographical Introduction*, 276.
24 John Colville, *Winston Churchill and His Inner Circle*, 24.

clubbable. For this reason, many notables were rejected from member-ship, including Lord Halifax and Clement Atlee.[25] The "Other Club" was intended to carve out a space of convivium and conversation above the strife of partisan debate, a place to practice friendship above and beyond politics. Most of its bylaws, read aloud at each gathering, were written by F. E. Smith, but Churchill allegedly wrote Rule Number 12, which summarizes the purpose of the club: "12. Nothing in the rules or inter-course of the Club shall interfere with the rancour or asperity of party politics."

The "Other Club" then was an attempt to cultivate a kind of friendship understood in the Aristotelian sense as a moral practice that transcends politics. Martin Gilbert explains that Churchill thought of all different forms of government, parliamentary democracy in particular was in need of such a higher practice: "An essential part of Churchill's political phi-losophy was his belief that nothing, even in the bitterest of political con-troversies, must be allowed to damage the fabric of the society as a whole. It was his strong conviction that within the democratic system political disagreements, whether inside or across party, must not entail personal animosities. Such animosities would, he believed, themselves endanger the democratic process."[26] For example, James Muller notes how Churchill, in *My Early Life*, notices how Parliament was a "'dueling-ground where although the business might be ruthless, and the weapons loaded with ball, there was ceremonious personal courtesy and mutual re-spect.' The young man was struck by the way that political opponents met socially for amicable conversation, and the contrast between the 'incredibly fierce,' 'blunt or even savage things' that Lord Randolph said to his fellow parliamentarians in politics, where frankness was required for free debate, and the hospitality of the welcome he gave them at home."[27]

Churchill understood the challenge facing parliamentary democracy along lines similar to the way of thinkers, including James Madison, who

25 Colin R. Coote, *The Other Club*, 31 n.1.
26 Gilbert, *Churchill's Political Philosophy*, 101–02.
27 James Muller, "Churchill's Understanding of Politics," 296, citing Churchill, *My Early Life: A Roving Commission* (London: Thornton But-terworth Limited, 1930), 48. Muller cites this edition instead of the 1958 edition referred here throughout.

believe parliamentary or liberal democracy cannot depend on forms and procedures alone ("ambition counteracting ambition") to generate civic and moral virtue. Parliamentary or liberal democracy depends on virtues that it cannot generate through the political process alone. For Churchill, the personal friendships practiced among the clubbable men of the "Other Club" would serve as a way of reinforcing the political friendship of Great Britain.

Even so, Churchill's endeavor to emphasize friendship and convivium over partisanship and politics cannot be pushed too far. Especially among upper-class members of the Conservative Party, politics was understood to be conducted among close lines of friendship and kin, which frequently meant those private ties took precedence over partisan politics and the public good. According to biographer Roy Jenkins, Churchill, the outsider who graduated from Harrow instead of Eton, "endeavored to rise above this by firmly taking the view that the discharge of public duty should neither be inhibited by nor impair private friendship."[28]

The "Other Club" would serve as a reminder that there is something greater for human beings than politics in the usual sense of the term, while that "something greater" would also serve politics in the larger sense. Churchill explained it best in a July 1933 speech at the "Other Club" about his friend, General Jan Smuts:

> This Club was born in the years before the war when faction ran high. Yet behind the cheers of the shouting crowds and the war cries of faction, we considered secretly all the great unities which combine Englishmen together in the face of common danger. When we think of the mighty empires that have been overthrown, of the governments that have disappeared, of the vast alterations in our social life, the change in manners, the change in morals—one might almost say everything has changed, yet here is our little Club, our small connection where we have had so many pleasant dinners, where we have talked with such complete indiscretion and no one

28   Jenkins, *Churchill: A Biography*, 471.

has ever been subject to the slightest annoyance for it, where there has been good fellowship and a spirit of growing association – we have weathered all winds and storms.[29]

The "Other Club" was a place of freedom, of giving, of free conversation and friendship.

Colin Coote explains, "the prototype of a dining club, such as the Other Club, is found among the early Christians in what was called an Eranos—literally 'love feast', but with no Bacchanalian undertones. It was a gathering to which each contributed something—a bottle party or, if that be too irreverent a title, a Dutch picnic."[30] Indeed for Coote, the prototype goes even farther back in history, and plays a significant role in humanity's permanent struggle for peace over strife, and leisure over necessity that was so crucial for Churchill's self-understanding:

> Even the pre-historic tribe was a sort of Club, dining together in some safe cave, while the dinosaurs prowled and roared— if that was the noise they made—outside. And even if the trappings of companionship, the cadence of good talk, the contacts of fine minds, the clash of verbal conflicts, should be temporarily swamped by banality or brutishness, the theme and refrain of civilization will break through again and be heard. For the song was wordless, the singing will never be done.[31]

Coote's prosaic summary of the "Other Club" experience emphasizes friendship over enmity and partisanship, giving over taking, conversation over bodily appetite, leisure over necessity, peace over strife, rest over exertion and work. It is the epitome of civilization, whose

---

29 Coote, *The Other Club*, 77.
30 Coote, *The Other Club*, 5. This was not the only attempt to recreate the Eranos experience in Europe during this time. See Tilo Schabert, "Introduction: The Eranos Experience," 9–20.
31 Coote, *The Other Club*, 149.

"wordless . . . singing will never be done." It is, in the words of Odysseus cited in the epigraph of this chapter, "the best life can offer."

The ethic that formed the "Other Club" also formed much of Churchill's life and political career. In her study of Churchill's dinner table diplomacy and policy-making, Cita Stelzer uses this statement by Leon Kass on the moral and intellectual and spiritual goods of dinner and conversation to summarize Churchill's ethic of friendship in statecraft:

> So too with friendship, whose beginnings are made possible by dinner, the shared meal itself grounds our being together. Amiability and friendliness are required and shared around the table. But it is the community of stories and conversation that is true communion. Fellow diners get to know each other's minds and hearts, even though no one is explicitly baring his soul or trafficking in personal matters. We are drawn to those whose tastes and tales we find admirable and charming. We arrange to dine with them again on another occasion.[32]

The second part of Kass's statement elaborates the moral and intellectual context of dinnertime conversation:

> Unlike the specifically philosophical friendship, with minds joined in the shared pursuit of wisdom, the aesthetic friendship of good taste celebrates the complete psychosomatic grown-togetherness that is the human being. At the same time the enlivened mind is free to reflect, often well after dinner is over, on the deeper meaning of a well-told tale or even on the splendid variety of human types that one has "tasted" while at the dining table. The generous and philanthropic hospitality of the gracious host and the nimble wit of the

---

32 Cita Stelzer, *Dinner With Churchill: Policy-Making at the Dinner Table*, 11, quoting Leon Kass, *The Hungry Soul: Eating and the Perfecting of Our Nature*, 182.

charming guest, all warmly remembered, enlarge our hearts and minds and beckon us toward friendship.[33]

Stelzer's study provides a useful overview of the centrality of conversation, story-telling, playfulness, face-to-face and personal contact, and even friendship in Churchill's statecraft. There he and his guests frequently replayed battles using salt shakers and cutlery for battalions, while he blew his cigar smoke like battle smoke.[34] He took special care for the choice of food and drink, as well as determining where guests would sit, including sitting enemies and rivals next to one another so that the convivium of the occasion could leaven their enmity and rivalry.[35]

His dinners blended the convivium of friendship with the serious concern over political matters. Throughout his life, Churchill regarded face-to-face meetings as the most important and effective way of conducting politics. One had to get to know the person to perform the work of politics. He says of Marlborough that "[o]ften in the casual remarks of great men one learns their true mind in an intimate way."[36] He understood high diplomacy involves the practice of vicarious friendship with other statesmen.[37] Churchill had a reputation of dominating conversations, but David Dilks observes too that he was a better listener than he appeared.[38] Churchill frequently invited England's top experts on various topics so he could gain insight into the latest political, scientific, and military developments. Dinners also served his personal diplomacy: "His curiosity led him to want to know, first-hand, what his negotiating partners were like; his self-confidence led him to believe that face-to-face

---

33 Kass, *The Hungry Soul*, 182. On this "psychosomatic grown-togetherness," see Immanuel Kant's discussion of having a good meal in good company as the "highest moral-physical good" ("Anthropology From a Pragmatic Point of View," 377–82).

34 Stelzer, *Dinner With Churchill*, 19–20.

35 Stelzer, *Dinner With Churchill*, 30.

36 Churchill, *Marlborough*, vol. 2, 225. See also ibid., 70.

37 For details on vicarious friendship in statecraft, see my "Friendship as Precondition and Consequence of Creativity in Politics."

38 David Dilks, *Churchill and Company*, 55.

meetings, the less formal the better, were the perfect occasions in which to deploy his skills."[39]

While Churchill joked, "if only I could dine with Stalin once a week, there would be no trouble at all,"[40] he certainly recognized the constraints that national and political interests placed upon the free play of convivium at these meals. He explained this point to the House of Commons: "It certainly would be most foolish to imagine that there is any chance of making straightaway a general settlement of all the cruel problems that exist in the East as well as the West . . . by personal meetings, however friendly."[41] In his Introduction to Stelzer's study, Andrew Roberts captures the blend of friendship and statecraft at these dinners: "He would turn mealtimes into information-exchange seminars, international summits, intelligence-gathering operations, gossip-fests, speech-practice sessions and even semi-theatrical performances. It must have been thrilling to have been present."[42]

Conversations and Story-Telling

In his Introduction to a recent edition of Churchill's *Thoughts and Adventures*, which includes essays published mostly during the 1930s, Muller explains that the articles "were usually rehearsed during dinner at Chartwell, his country seat, where he liked to surround himself with stimulating company . . . . Reading these essays is like being invited to dinner at Chartwell, where the soup was limpid, Pol Roger Champagne flowed, the pudding had a theme, and Churchill entertained lucky visitors with vivid conversation."[43] Muller illuminates the close link between

---

39 Stelzer, *Dinner With Churchill*, 4–5. Stelzer cites Churchill's telegraph to Roosevelt in October 1944 where he tells him, "I feel certain that personal contact is essential" (ibid., 36).
40 Stelzer, *Dinner With Churchill*, 10, citing Martin Gilbert, *Road to Victory, 1941–1945*, volume 7 of *Winston S. Churchill*, 664.
41 Stelzer, *Dinner With Churchill*, 2–3, quoting Churchill to the House of Commons, November 3, 1953.
42 Andrew Roberts, "Introduction," in Stelzer, *Dinner With Churchill*, xiv.
43 James Muller, "Introduction," in Churchill, *Thoughts and Adventures*, viii, x–xi.

conversation and Churchill's writing. His conversations pointed beyond themselves and his writings were conversational. The writings reflect the form of conversation in a way that resembles somewhat the manner in which some of the great ethical and political writings of the past have conversation as their form: Platonic dialogues, Aristotle's *Nicomachean Ethics*, and the *Summa Theologiae* by St. Thomas Aquinas, to name a few.

Churchill's writings do not rise to the level of philosophical sophistication of these writings. However, he seems to share their insight that writing is a form of story-telling about life, which is embodied best as conversation, the quintessential activity of friends. Indeed, Churchill seems to agree with Aristotle's observation that:

> [O]ne's being is choiceworthy on account of the awareness of oneself as being good, and such an awareness is pleasant in itself. Therefore one also ought to share in a friend's awareness that he *is* (or share his friend's consciousness of his existence (*sunaisthanesthai hoti estin*)), and this would come through living together and sharing conversation and thinking; for this would seem to be what living together means in the case of human beings.[44]

For Aristotle, as for Churchill, human life is crowned by "living together and sharing conversation and thinking." For most of us, this takes the form of sharing stories of our experiences with our friends. We act together with our friends, and our friendship and shared action is made sweeter by recollecting those actions by talking about them, by sharing stories. This crowning experience also has something visionary about it. Together, we friends behold and pursue the good and the beautiful while beholding each other. Just as binocular vision has greater depth than

---

44 Aristotle, *Nicomachean Ethics*, 1170b10–12. Emphasis added. Muller cites this passage to explain the importance of conversation and friendship for Churchill (Muller, "Introduction," in Churchill, *Great Contemporaries*, xiii, n.13). For elaboration of Aristotle's insight, see my *The Form of Politics: Aristotle and Plato on Friendship*, chapters 1 and 2.

monocular vision, so too friends enhance each other's knowledge of the world and of themselves. Following Aristotle, I shall refer to this vision-ary crowning experience of friendship as "sunaisthesis," literally mean-ing, "shared perception."

Eva Brann writes a poignant aphorism that expresses this truth: "We save up the events of our days to tell our friends, feeling that until our affairs have been told they haven't quite happened: Thus do our friends confirm our lives."[45] Indeed, Brann's aphorism indicates that our actions together with friends are not fully complete until "our affairs have been told." Story-telling completes action, and our "living together and shar-ing conversation and thinking" is a moral practice, not only of acting and then sharing stories: in sharing our stories that include our friends our lives become intertwined. We share our stories in the deep sense that our lives together *are* our stories. This is the moral and political vision that animates Churchill, the great statesman, great friend to other states-men, and great author. Political action is conducted by great individuals whose actions are made more effectual and sweeter by being accompa-nied by equally great friends who can share in the adventure, and then of telling stories of those actions in order to complete their meaning.

For Aristotle, such shared conversation consists in its highest form as philosophical contemplation. While not a philosopher in the strict sense because he was a statesman and man of action, Churchill's con-versations had a philosophical dimension to them insofar as they were shared inquiries into the truth of practical matters. They were what might be regarded as exercises in practical political philosophizing, with the aim of determining what should be done, the central question of political science since Aristotle.

Moreover, I shall demonstrate that some of his major historical writ-ings, most notably his biography of Marlborough, are in fact inquiries into first principles of political action. They are examples of "moral his-tory" because their portrayal of human actions reveal the morality of the characters of the main actors. As such, Churchill's vision of conversation, story-telling, of the relationship of thought and action, of politics to

---

45 Eva Brann, *Open Secrets/Inward Prospects: Reflections on World and Soul,* 51.

reflection upon politics, reflects the manner in which statesmen and philosophers historically have regarded them—as moral and political practices where friendship is situated at the core.

As suggested in Coote's comment about cavemen sharing convivium while wild animals roamed outside their cave, this vision of human life and of politics as story-telling reaches far back in human history. One early articulation of this way of life can be seen in Book IX of the *Odyssey*, quoted at the beginning of this chapter. There Homer portrays Odysseus in the palace of the Phaikians. After listening to Demodocus sing of his, Odysseus's, travails, and before Odysseus proceeds to tell his own tale, he proclaims to King Alcinous that the "crown of life" is listening to the bard while banqueting. It is noteworthy that Aristotle cites part of Odysseus's statement as evidence that "those of earlier times," the Homeric heroes, regarded banqueting and listening to the bard as the "pastime (*diagoge*) of free persons."[46] One might say that such story-telling is political friendship brought to form.

In his actions and writings, Churchill embodied political friendship as story-telling.

Boris Johnson recently argued that Winston Churchill's "ethic was really pre-Christian, even Homeric. His abiding interest was in glory and prestige—both for himself and for the 'British empire.' But he had a deep sense of what it was right and fitting for him to do—and remember his self-narrator's eye was beadily following and judging him all the time."[47] While Johnson exaggerates Churchill's Homeric ethic at the expense of the Christian elements that formed his ethic, all of the elements of politics as story-telling are contained in this statement. Churchill had the virtue of magnanimity (*megalapsychia*), the paramount virtue of the statesman. Johnson's label of him as a "self-narrator" reflects how Churchill conceived of political action—his political action most notably—as a story, indeed, as an epic.[48] Just as Odysseus sings of his own actions, so too was Churchill the singer of his own actions, and indeed,

---

46 Aristotle, *Politics* 1338a14, 23–24.
47 Boris Johnson, *The Churchill Factor*, 113.
48 For details of this side of Churchill, see Jonathan Rose, *The Literary Churchill*.

of his own people. Reviewing in the *New Republic* a volume of Churchill's speeches, *Blood, Sweat, and Tears*, Malcolm Cowley proclaimed: "He not only makes laws for his people but writes their songs as well, in the sense that his speeches are battle cries, dirges for the fallen and hymns of victory."[49] For Churchill, friendship and the capacity for conversation – sharing good cheer and feasting—was the mark of a worthy companion. John Colville explained that "those with whom it is agreeable to dine" were fit to be Churchill's companions. Like Odysseus, Churchill's moral vision of politics consisted of performing great deeds with great friends, and then telling stories about their adventures (or writing books about them)—singing songs "for those yet to be born," as the Phaikian king explains to Odysseus the purpose of action. Indeed, Churchill's Cabinet ministers sometimes complained that it seemed everything Churchill did throughout the war was performed with an eye to write it up in the book that became *The Second World War*.

We turn in the next chapter to how Churchill regarded his friends and political associates as his fellow-adventurers, sharing adventure and conversation.

---

49   Malcolm Cowley, "Mr. Churchill Speaks," 537.

Chapter Two
Great Friends and Friends Who Are Great

A competent politician and trained speaker in the shape of one Aaron would be provided. Moses now remembered his kinsman Aaron, with whom he had been good friends before he had to flee to Egypt. Thereupon action![1]

Great Contemporaries and Great Friends

Churchill recounts the "pastime of free persons" in his *Great Contemporaries*, a collection of essays on many English but also non-English politicians, statesmen, and men of letters. Subjects include former Prime Ministers Joseph Chamberlain and Stanley Baldwin; Adolf Hitler and Franklin Roosevelt; and Rudyard Kipling and T. E. Lawrence. The standard of conduct that Churchill applies in judging their greatness is their capacity for conversation and friendship: those with whom it is agreeable to dine. Indeed, Muller, the editor of the most recent edition of *Great Contemporaries*, observes that friendship is a key theme of the work: "Aristotle tells us that the characteristic activity of friendship is conversation, and nothing is taken more seriously in *Great Contemporaries*, which reads like a series of conversations between the author and his 'gentle reader.'"[2]

Churchill's essay on F. E. Smith, First Earl of Birkenhead, is poignant in this regard. It was a memorial to his best friend, who died in 1930, and

---

1   Churchill, "Moses: The Leader of a People," in *Thoughts and Adventures*, 305.
2   Muller, "Introduction," *Great Contemporaries*, xii–xiii, citing *Nicomachean Ethics* 1170b, the focal text for Aristotle's discussion of "sunaisthetic" friendship that is central to this study.

the entire volume of *Great Contemporaries* seems to have been inspired by Smith's own volume, *Contemporary Personalities,* which had been published in 1924.[3] John Colville observes Churchill "never had a truer, cleverer or more congenial friend" than Smith.[4] David Dilks argues that Churchill never again had a such a true friend as Smith, which was reflected in his view that the generation of English statesmen in the 1930s was of lower stature than Smith and the "great contemporaries" covered in *Great Contemporaries.*[5] Churchill's wife, Clementine, who disliked Smith, told Smith's widow that he had wept for his friend and said several times, "I feel so lonely."[6] And so it seemed for the rest of his life, at least until World War Two: "This conviction—that the people amongst whom he spent a good part of his later political life were of a lesser order than the giants of his youth and early manhood—was openly proclaimed. It explains a good deal about Churchill's relations with colleagues, and his detachment from the mainstream of British political life in the 1930s . . . . Politics, he said, were not what they had been. The level was lower."[7] Indeed, Beaverbrook and Jan Smuts were Churchill's only intimate friends after Birkenhead died.[8]

David Freeman suggests that in Smith and Churchill, there was never such a dynamic friendship in all of British history:

> The friendship between Churchill and F. E. Smith was not only the strongest that Churchill ever had, but virtually his only one based on a shared sense of equality. With Lloyd George, Churchill always felt the inferior, just as he occupied the superior role in his association with Brendan Bracken. With Max Beaverbrook there was always a certain friction, with Roosevelt there was a clear distance. But Winston and F.E. could share all their thoughts and wisdom, with the knowledge that each would receive a valuable experience.[9]

3   Muller, "Introduction," xxxi. F. E. Smith, *Contemporary Personalities.*
4   Colville, *Winston Churchill and His Inner Circle,* 19.
5   David Dilks, *Churchill and Company,* 14 and 26.
6   Dilks, *Churchill and Company,* 26.
7   Dilks, *Churchill and Company,* 14.
8   A. J. P. Taylor, *Beaverbrook,* 411.
9   David Freeman, "The Friendship Between Churchill and F. E. Smith."

In later chapters, we shall examine the friendship of Churchill with Beaverbrook and with Roosevelt. Freeman's unfavorable comparison of his later friendships with that of Smith may well be true, but, as we shall see, genuine goodwill and love characterized those later friendships as well.

In his essay on Smith, Churchill writes in memoriam:

> It was only after the Parliament of 1906 had run some months of its course that we were introduced to one another by a common friend as we stood at the bar of the House of Commons before an important division. But from that hour our friendship was perfect. It was one of my most precious possessions. It was never disturbed by the fiercest party fighting. It grew stronger as nearly a quarter of a century slipped by, and it lasted till his untimely death. The pleasure and instruction of his companionship were of the highest order.[10]

His essay recounts highlights of their friendship, Smith's remarkable wit (of which Churchill feared being the target), "canine virtues" of "courage, fidelity, vigilance, and love of the chase," and of course his remarkable conversation which he judges on par with the older generation of statesmen including Balfour, Morley, Asquith, Rosebery, and Lloyd George. Freeman points out the primary example of Smith's "canine virtues" was his constancy in supporting Churchill after the disastrous Dardanelles campaign that for a while severely damaged Churchill's political career. Even Clementine regarded Smith's actions during the Dardanelles crisis as a sign of a true friend. Even so, Smith's "canine virtues" do not mean he was a mere follower of Churchill. They were equals, as Churchill's awe (and fear) of Smith's wit indicates. These virtues enabled Churchill and Smith to carry on their friendship in a manner that transcended politics while also sustaining their political alliance. This capacity of maintaining the "English tradition of not bringing politics into private life"[11] is a constant thread throughout the essays

---

10   Churchill, "'F. E.' First Earl of Birkenhead," in *Great Contemporaries*, 172.
11   Churchill, "Joseph Chamberlain," in *Great Contemporaries*, 76.

in *Great Contemporaries*, and it is the standard by which he criticizes them when they fail to uphold that standard.

As seen in the previous chapter with Churchill's dinnertime diplomacy, conversation is not simply an escape from politics but is its very form. Indeed, he saw a connection between the capacity for conversation and genuine political prudence. He criticizes Herbert Henry Asquith for communing "deeply within himself" less than most other statesmen, which diminished his capacity for political prudence:

> Many things are learnt by those who live their whole lives with their main work; and although it is a great gift at once to have an absorbing interest and to be able to throw it off in lighter hours, it seemed at times that Asquith threw it off too easily, too completely. He drew so strict a line between Work and Play that one might almost think work had ceased to attract him . . . . The case was settled and put aside; judgment was formed, was delivered, and did not require review.[12]

Churchill appreciated the distinction, drawn by premodern philosophers, between the life of contemplation and the life of action. He once remarked that "a man's Life must be nailed to a cross either of Thought or Action."[13] However, he recognized that in choosing the life of action, one can never really escape one's chosen lot nor easily throw it off. For a statesman, moments of leisure will always be tied to action; the thoughts and conversations in moments of leisure will eventually percolate toward action. The best deliberations seem to be those done from being habituated in active leisuring, in the sense Aristotle describes such activity.[14] Statesmen, nailed to the cross of "Action," lack the freedom to keep such leisuring too far from practical affairs. However, their concern for practical affairs must also be influenced by the spirit of leisuring. Churchill's point here seems to be that Asquith never let habits of playful conversation inform his political deliberations, nor did politics for him

12 Churchill, "Herbert Henry Asquith," in *Great Contemporaries*, 141.
13 Churchill, *My Early Life, 1874–1904*, 113.
14 See *Politics* 1334a12–25.

resemble play as it did for Churchill. Drawing "so strict a line between Work and Play" made his political deliberations inadequate and his conclusions too certain. One must approach the life of action in a spirit of playfulness that takes the form of conversation and friendship, and which also helps inform one's political prudence.[15]

Asquith's "limitation" was that, in English philosopher Michael Oakeshott's terms, he was a "rationalist." He had geometric concepts and categories which "did not require review," that he applied when confronting political affairs. This is not political prudence, which Churchill describes in contrast to Asquith's approach:

> The world, nature, human beings do not move like machines. The edges are never clear-cut, but always frayed. Nature never draws a line without smudging it. Conditions are so variable, episodes so unexpected, experiences so conflicting, that flexibility of judgment and a willingness to assume a somewhat humbler attitude towards external phenomena may well play their part in the equipment of a modern Prime Minister.[16]

Few statements on the nature of political prudence come closer to Aristotle's understanding of *phronesis* as the type of wisdom that is found in our actions in particular circumstances. It is opposite to the top-down imposition of categories that characterizes the rationalist like Asquith.

Churchill makes a similar observation when contrasting the "American mind" from the British:

> In the military as in the commercial or production spheres the American mind runs naturally to broad, sweeping, logical conclusions on the largest scale. It is on these that they build their practical thought and action. They feel that once the

---

15 See Johannes Huizinga, *Homo Ludens: A Study of the Play-Element in Culture*, ch. 5.

16 Churchill, "Herbert Henry Asquith," in *Great Contemporaries*, 137.

foundation has been planned on true and comprehensive lines all other stages will follow naturally and almost inevitably. The British mind does not work quite in this way. We do not think that logic and clear-cut principles are necessarily the sole keys to what ought to be done in swiftly changing and indefinable situations. In war particularly we assign a larger importance to opportunism and improvisation, seeking rather to live and conquer in accordance with the unfolding event than to aspire to dominate it often by fundamental decisions.[17]

Like Alexis de Tocqueville, who characterized the American mind as a form of "Cartesian" rationalism, Churchill contrasted practical wisdom with rationalism that deduces actions from "logic and clear-cut principles."[18]

Churchill also saw a connection between political prudence or *phronesis* and conversation and friendship. In conversation, things are always in flux; it is a back-and-forth of discussion between partners. Nothing is settled and no conclusions are drawn. Conversation, though freer and more leisured than political deliberation, is an image of political life where nothing also is settled and contestation and debate are permanent. The capacity to converse makes one better suited for political deliberation. Oakeshott pinpoints the essence of conversation:

Conversation is not an enterprise designed to yield an extrinsic profit, a contest where a winner gets a prize, nor is it an activity of exegesis; it is an unrehearsed intellectual adventure. It is with conversation as with gambling, its significance lies neither in winning nor in losing, but in wagering. Properly speaking, it is impossible in the absence of a diversity of voices: in it different universes of discourse meet, acknowledge each other and enjoy an oblique relationship which

17 Churchill, *The Second World War*, vol. 3, 596–97.
18 See Tocqueville, *Democracy in America*, 403.

neither requires nor forecasts their being assimilated to one another.[19]

Being a good conversationalist entails submitting oneself to this wager and letting things be as they are. Such an attitude enables one better to exercise political prudence that sees the variability of nature and its conflicting circumstances, and to tolerate its smudging. To converse is to inhabit a community shared with others. It is to view oneself as a partner in adventure, and as a friend. Indeed, while Churchill was domineering and difficult with his War Cabinet, its members were sufficiently resilient to bear and resist him.[20]

Magnanimity and Friendship

Churchill's point about nature smudging its lines serves as a helpful reminder when considering another important element of his understanding of friendship and politics. It is noteworthy that Churchill's "response" to Smith's book, *Contemporary Personalities*, was to write a book called *Great Contemporaries*. The book is a response to a conversation he partook in with his best friend. Churchill of course was keenly interested in political greatness and his book is a testament of sorts to what he learned about the subject from the greats of his father's generation. Part of Churchill's sadness in losing Smith was that his death also seemed to mark the end of a generation of great personalities in British politics. Churchill was concerned not only with having great friends, but also with having friends who are great.

However, in the view of many scholars and observers of history, greatness, or magnanimity, seems to incline to solitude, not

19 Michael Oakeshott, "The Voice of Poetry in the Conversation of Mankind," *Rationalism in Politics*, 490. Churchill liked to gamble and he also liked to play poker with his good friend Beaverbrook, who always won (Schneer, *Ministers at War: Winston Churchill and His War Cabinet*, 176). See also Stephen Miller's evocation of conversation as the center of civilized life (*Conversation: A History of a Declining Art*).

20 See Schneer, *Ministers at War: Winston Churchill and His War Cabinet*, 109.

friendship.[21] Monuments to great statesmen typically portray them as individuals. There are many statues of Churchill alone. There is only one statue of Churchill and Roosevelt conversing together (it is on Bond Street in London). There are few great men, which means there are even fewer great men's friendships. Moreover, great men typically aim for goals that few can actually see and therefore share, and their ambitions make them difficult to get along with. Can great men be friends with anyone? Can they only be genuine friends with other great men? To what extent do they need or desire friendship with other great men?

Aristotle seems to suggest that friendship is not really a concern for the magnanimous statesman. The magnanimous man is preoccupied with performing great deeds. He "does favors but is ashamed to have them done for him, since the former belongs to one who is superior, but the latter to one who has someone superior to him"; and he "is not capable of leading his life to suit anyone else, other than a friend."[22] The magnanimous man prizes his autonomy and his capacity to provide great benefits to others. He has few friends because few individuals are worthy of his greatness. They just get in the way of his desire to bestow favors. Thus it might be said he is less interested in friendship (which implies being loved in addition to loving) than in having others recognize his greatness and authority. He seeks admiration, not love. Alexander the Great, the emperor, seems to be the political incarnation of Aristotle's magnanimous man.[23]

Although Aristotle's description of the magnanimous man seems to paint him as aloof, possibly arrogant and self-absorbed, the reality is that the magnanimous man is a supreme friend, at least to those who can reach him.[24] The magnanimous man seeks not just honour

21 Will Morrissey provides a useful overview of Churchill's magnanimity but says little about how it fits with the importance he placed upon friendship ("The Statesman as Great-Souled Man: Winston Churchill," 197–220).

22 Aristotle, *Nicomachean Ethics*, 1124b9–11, 1125a1.

23 See Harry Jaffa, "Foreword" to Kirk Emmert, *Winston S. Churchill on Empire*, ix; Alexandre Kojève, "Tyranny and Wisdom," in Leo Strauss, *On Tyranny*, 141–45, 169–72.

24 For discussion of magnanimity and friendship, see Suzanne Stern-Gillet, "Souls Great and Small: Aristotle on Self-Knowledge, Friendship, and Civic Engagement," 51–86.

or recognition, but he also loves because loving is superior to honour because of, in part at least, the superiority of friendship to political life.[25]

Churchill's recognition that love and friendship are superior to honour is most clearly seen in the honour he paid to his great enemy, General Erwin Rommel, whom he seemed to regard a military genius. He respected and admired Rommel, as one can with one's mortal enemy.[26] But emphatically he did not love him. Political friendship suggests love is superior to honour in the minds of statesmen. Indeed, the friendships of those performing great deeds necessarily involve spirited debate and quarrel, which reflects the dynamism of the magnanimous characters as well as the importance they place upon the great purposes for which they act. This fractiousness is most apparent among those performing acts of statesmanship, like those performed by Churchill. Once achieved, his friendships are more important than anything else. As we saw in Chapter One, Churchill's fear of Lord Birkenhead's wit constituted part of his loving him. We shall see in Chapter Three how his spirited quarrels and antagonisms with Lord Beaverbrook constituted an integral part of his love for him as well. We shall see in Chapters Four and Five how the challenges of navigating political differences with Roosevelt constituted an integral part of his loving him. The magnanimous man loves a good fight with his magnanimous friends. He loves them as worthy combatants, and their greatness as individuals and as friends consists in their capacity to bring out his own greatness.

Churchill seemed to need and desire friendships with other great men, which, he knew with regret, were rare. It is noteworthy that many of his contemporaries summarized Churchill's character as "magnanimous." Beaverbrook once asked himself what was Churchill's chief

25 Aristotle, *Nicomachean Ethics*, VIII.8.
26 In January 1942, Churchill paid tribute to him in a speech to the House of Commons after Rommel committed suicide, by Hitler's order, as punishment for taking part in a conspiracy against Hitler. Churchill calls him a "great general" and expresses admiration of him for hating Hitler. Churchill notes the "reproaches from the public" he received for his tribute: "Still, I do not regret or retract the tribute I paid to Rommel, unfashionable though it was judged (*The Second World War*, vol. 3, 176–77).

virtue. "Magnanimity," he answered.[27] This seems to be something like Churchill's own view of himself, as he claims "magnanimity in victory" as the epigraph and moral of his *The Second World War*.[28] And as Leo Strauss claimed on the day after Churchill died, Churchill was a "magnanimous statesman" whose "greatness" lay in his great deeds, including his "heroic action on behalf of human freedom."[29]

Biographers like Jon Meacham and contemporaries like Lord Chandos identify Churchill's magnanimity with his capacity to overlook and forgive insults, apparently rooted in the manner he learned to cope with his stern father who never appeared to approve of him.[30]

Lord Chandos also saw Churchill's magnanimity in his capacity to enjoy political conflict as a conflict between ideas and not between people, which reinforces the view that for Churchill, politics involves a degree of elevating one's gaze to higher human ends and purposes. Churchill's magnanimity can also be seen in his claim that he only hated Germany until it was defeated. According to Violet Bonham Carter, "He never sought to trample on a fallen foe, whether a political opponent or a defeated nation . . . . His enmity could not survive once victory was won. He never hated nations or men as such. He only hated their ideas. He would knock a man down in order to pick him up again in a better frame of mind."[31] Indeed, touring the ruins while at the Potsdam conference in 1945, he was overcome with compassion for the "haggard" bombed-out Berliners.[32] He also tried to protect the German civilians caught behind Soviet lines near the end of the war.[33] Churchill's attitude

27 Meacham, *Franklin and Winston*, 30.
28 "In defeat, defiance; in war, resolution; in victory, magnanimity; in peace, goodwill." Epigraph, *The Second World War*. Andrew Roberts suggests the beatitudes are the inspiration for the epigraph ("Winston Churchill and Religion—A Comfortable Relationship with the Almighty"). See also Jonathan Sandys and Wallace Henley, *God and Churchill*, 94–100.
29 Strauss, "Churchill's Greatness." See also Strauss's comment that he learned what Aristotle meant by magnanimity by studying Churchill (letter to Löwith).
30 Meacham, *Franklin and Winston*, 30.
31 Quoted in Meacham, *Franklin and Winston*, 30.
32 Stelzer, *Dinner With Churchill: Policy-Making at the Dinner Table*, 221.
33 Churchill, *The Second World War*, vol. 6, 567–74.

was similar to that of Lincoln, who invoked "charity for all" in his Second Inaugural and of whom it was said that he was the South's greatest friend because of his desire to rehabilitate and reconstruct it instead of punish it at the conclusion of the war.

In calling Churchill magnanimous, observers focused on the part of magnanimity that involves Churchill's capacity to overlook insults, his lack of "rancour" as Beaverbrook noticed.[34] They recognized he was able to do this because he focused upon matters greater than personal ego and ambition. Magnanimity focuses upon the common good. This is consistent with Aristotle's description of the magnanimous man: "Nor is he apt to bear grudges, for it is not characteristic of one who is great-souled to remember things against anyone, not of any sort and especially not wrongs, but rather to overlook them."[35] Aristotle's description of the magnanimous man is frequently regarded as describing someone arrogant instead of exhibiting the virtues that Churchill exhibited. For instance, in the *Posterior Analytics* Aristotle claims, citing Achilles as his example, that the magnanimous man in fact does not tolerate insults.[36] This claim appears to conflict with the one just quoted, but this impasse is cleared if we pay attention to the protreptic rhetoric of the *Nicomachean Ethics* whereby Aristotle takes common understandings of virtues and refines them to bring it under the rule of reason. In the case of magnanimity, one can discern that his discussion is to show that though the magnanimous man is concerned with honour as the greatest external good, it is still only a mere *external* good and that his ambition to be worthy of "great things" properly means a desire for truth. Honour becomes "a small thing."[37] He therefore appears arrogant to those who are not magnanimous. Aristotle sees the magnanimous man generally as having a conflicted soul inasmuch as he is motivated both by honour and by truth. His protreptic teaching is meant not so much to have truth win out, but at least to have the desire for honour serve the desire for truth.

---

34 Young, *Churchill and Beaverbrook*, 45.
35 Aristotle, *Nicomachean Ethics*, 1125a2–4.
36 Aristotle, *Posterior Analytics*, 97b14–26.
37 See *Nicomachean Ethics* 1123b3–4 and 1124a18–20 and Joe Sachs's editorial notes that accompany these texts (nn. 85–88).

Only then can the magnanimous man genuinely be worthy of the great things for which he aims. This can occur only when he recognizes the manner in which loving truly is superior to honour, which would be, it seems, when the statesman risks the entirety of his honour for the sake of right, and when the good of his people takes precedence over his own honour.[38] In addition to his own virtue-friendships and the demands the political friendship of Great Britain placed upon him, Churchill's own recognition of this "purified" magnanimity can be seen in his attitude toward losing the 1945 election, and in the manner in which he regarded the outcome of World War Two as "tragic." Having gone to war on a point of honour (defending Poland), the war ended in dishonour and the prospect of an even greater danger facing the West. Churchill concludes *The Second World War* by noting he is merely a "servant" of his people who had ousted him as their leader, and implicitly, despite appearances and despite their public celebrations of war's apparent end, that he indeed had not saved them. Only when the statesman recognizes that truth is higher than honour, can his magnanimity be said to be an "adornment" (*kosmos*) of the virtues.[39]

Magnanimity and Christian Ethics

The focus of many commentators and contemporaries on Churchill's capacity to overlook insults or to forgive emphasize one aspect of magnanimity. By emphasizing his magnanimous capacity to forgive, they are imbued by what Churchill called the "flame of Christian ethics."[40] His magnanimity enabled him to forgive injustices and insults against him. While Churchill's relationship to the Christian faith is ambiguous, it

38   See Aristotle, *Nicomachean Ethics*, VIII.8.

39   Aristotle, *Nicomachean Ethics*, 1124a2. The argument of the *Nicomachean Ethics* posits magnanimity as the first peak or crown of the moral life that brings into focus the necessity that all the virtues be present. The others are found in his discussion of justice and of friendship. For details, see Robert Sokolowski, "Phenomenology of Friendship," 451–70.

40   Churchill, "The Flame of Christian Ethics, Speech At University Of Oslo, May 12, 1948," 7643–45. See also Havers, *Leo Strauss and Anglo-American Democracy*, 102–09.

would be a mistake to impute to this ambiguity a clear preference for so-called pagan ethics. Indeed, he consistently refrains from drawing such a sharp line between the two. When he seems to he generally does so to illuminate the limitation of a Christian ethic that has moved too far toward pacifism.[41]

This refrain can be seen in one of his most famous statements on the subject, his assessment of Chamberlain during the Munich crisis: "The Sermon on the Mount is the last word in ethics. Everyone respects the Quakers. Still, it is not on these terms that Ministers assume their responsibilities of guiding states."[42] "Meekness and humility" seem unreliable guides for statecraft, but:

> [T]here is however one helpful guide, namely, for a nation to keep its word and to act in accordance with its treaty obligations to allies. This guide is honour. It is baffling to reflect that what men call honour does not correspond always to Christian ethics. Honour is often influenced by that element of pride which plays so large a part in its inspiration. Here however the moment came when honour pointed the path of duty, and when also the right judgment of the facts at that time would have reinforced its dictates.[43]

Churchill here appears to choose "honour" or pagan magnanimity over "meekness and humility" as the virtue appropriate for the statesman.

41 Churchill seems to have intuited that the Sermon on the Mount is not ethics but the condition of ethics, which is the free gift or surrender of the self. Indeed he titles his discourse "The Flame of Christian Ethics" as a way of acknowledging the effects of the Sermon upon the ethical life while acknowledging the mystery of its source. On the Sermon's "deconstruction" of ethics, see David Walsh, *Politics of the Person as the Politics of Being*, 56–65.

42 Churchill, *The Second World War*, vol. 1, 287. Daniel J. Mahoney views Churchill's indictment of the appeasement policy as an "indictment of the easygoing acquiescence of democratic peoples" (*The Conservative Foundations of the Liberal Order*, 79–80). That is, in a Tocquevillian vein, it is due more to the "structure and habits of democratic peoples."

43 Churchill, *The Second World War*, vol. 1, 288.

However, a closer reading suggests a more complicated picture. The immediate context of these comments about the Munich crisis is practical wisdom. On one extreme, there are those "who are prone by temperament and character to seek sharp and clear-cut solutions of difficult and obscure problems, who are ready to fight whenever some challenge comes from a foreign Power, have not always been right." These people lack practical wisdom because they "seek sharp and clear-cut solutions"; as rationalists in the sense that Oakeshott uses the term, they fail to understand the insight Churchill expresses in his Asquith essay: "nature never draws a line without smudging it." They are also excessively spirited and lack caution. They are those whom Machiavelli says incline to impetuosity.

On the other extreme are "those whose inclination is to bow their heads, to seek patiently and faithfully for peaceful compromise" and who are "not always wrong. On the contrary, in the majority of instances they may be right, not only morally but from a practical standpoint. How many wars have been averted by patience and persisting goodwill!" There is something intrinsically good about this moral position, but taken to its extreme, as the pacifists of Great Britain did, leads to ruin and is moral evil. Their position would have contradicted the basic principle of statecraft that Churchill summarizes in his Marlborough biography: "One rule of conduct alone survives as a guide to men in their wanderings: fidelity to covenants, the honour of soldiers, and the hatred of causing human woe."[44]

For the most part, the impetuous are wrong and for the most part, the meek and humble are right. This in itself is a remarkable admission because it acknowledges the priority of mercy in ethics while also acknowledging that mercy extends beyond ethics, its condition as it were. This seems to be what Churchill means when he claims the Sermon on the Mount the "last word in ethics." However, in this particular case, the Munich crisis, a middle position between the two is needed, which is "honour." Indeed, Churchill regards "honour" generally as a "helpful guide." Yet while honour tends, like the impetuous, to perform "utterly vain and unreasonable deeds," the honour he has in mind points towards

44 Churchill, *Marlborough*, vol. 2, 996.

"the path of duty." Honour is good when it is a means of obtaining right, which it can do when it is moderated and guided by principle. As with magnanimity, honour can only be genuine when it serves the right moral and political principle.

Churchill's assessment of what was at stake with the Munich agreement indicates his view of what right principle was at work here. He cites Marshal Keitel's answer to a question put to him by the Czech representative at the Nuremberg trials: "The object of Munich (i.e., reaching an agreement at Munich) was to get Russia out of Europe, to gain time, and to complete the German rearmaments."[45] In "the majority of instances," "meekness and humility" temper the impetuous. In this particular case, this approach would have meant national and even international suicide, which is hardly the goal of the Sermon on the Mount. Indeed, stopping a maniacal totalitarian dictator like Hitler is the righteous action. Christian ethics does not conflict with honour in this case. If anything, its commitment to righteousness assists with tying honour to duty. Churchill was primarily concerned with possessing strength to perform right deeds. Humility, meekness, or mercy are not in themselves contrary to the practice of politics. As he told his mother, Jenny, in 1919, "The finest combination in the world is power and mercy. The worst combination in the world is weakness and strife." Again in his speech to the House of Commons on July 14, 1940, he declared, "We may show mercy—we shall ask for none."[46]

Churchill's magnanimity is gentler than that offered by Aristotle. Alternatively, his magnanimity is how Aristotle understood magnanimity to be at its very best. It is one whose perfection in many ways was enabled by the Christian culture that imbued it, both by tempering his own ambition, and by tempering the Western civilization that prizes forgiveness, not punishment, for insults and injustices against him.[47]

---

45 Churchill, *The Second World War*, vol. 1, 286.
46 Sandys and Henley, *God and Churchill*, 97.
47 On the harmony of magnanimity and Christian virtue, even humility, see Aquinas, *Summa Theologiæ*, II–II.129; Mary Keys, "Humility and Greatness of Soul"; Kenneth L. Deutsch, "Thomas Aquinas on Magnanimous and Prudent Statesmanship"; Joseph R. Fornieri, "Lincoln and Biblical Magnanimity."

This consideration of Churchill's magnanimity in light of Aristotle's teaching shows why the magnanimous man desires and needs friends. He needs assistance to achieve great deeds but, more than that, he needs a friend with whom to enjoy those deeds and with whom to share and recognize each other's virtues. His moral virtue may be complete but he is still not self-sufficient. He needs someone with whom to share his adornment.[48]

Statesmanship, Friendship, and Daimonism

Subsequent chapters will demonstrate Churchill's friendship in magnanimity. However, this Aristotelian category does not adequately capture the psychological complexity behind him and even his understanding of himself as friendly statesman. This greater complexity is found throughout his writings especially. His remarkable essay on Moses as political leader, published in *Thoughts and Adventures*, provides a glimpse into this greater complexity, which, following Aristotle's great teacher Plato, elucidates the "daimonism" or genius a great statesman needs.

In "Moses, Leader of a People," Churchill strives to capture what precisely made Moses so great. Throughout his life and in his writings,

---

48 Neither the magnanimous man nor the philosopher, Aristotle's two paradigms for human greatness—one active, the other contemplative—are solitary. If they were, Aristotle would regard the emperor the ideal statesman and the Stoic or Averroeistic sage the ideal philosopher. This is where Harry Jaffa's understanding of magnanimity errs when he claims Churchill's imperialism "follows closely the articulation of Aristotle's argument" ("Foreword" to Kirk Emmert, *Winston S. Churchill on Empire*, ix). Muller demurs by suggesting instead that "empire could advance civilization. There is a *distant echo* of Aristotle's account of despotic rule in the first book of the *Politics* in Churchill's suggestion that imperial rule is justified when it works to the benefit of both ruler and ruled" (James Muller, "Review: Imperialism as the Highest Stage of Civilization," 581 (emphasis added), review of Emmert, *Winston S. Churchill on Empire*). Instead, the friendliness of both the statesman and the philosopher is the result of the constitution of reason. For details, see my *The Form of Politics: Aristotle and Plato on Friendship*, ch. 2. I discuss how Churchill's imperialism relates to friendship below in Chapter Seven.

Churchill was fascinated with greatness or "genius." However, despite this fascination, it is noteworthy that other than his study of Marlborough, this is his only written assessment of a world historical figure (the figures covered in *Great Contemporaries* are either of lesser significance or, in the case of Hitler, are evil). Despite his admiration of Napoleon (he kept a bust of him), Churchill barely mentions him in his writings.

Churchill considers in Moses a mysterious quality of greatness that eludes Aristotle's treatment of magnanimity. It is a kind of daimonism or musical soul that Churchill sees in Moses' miracles and drive. Despite Churchill's discovery of it in Moses, it is a much-discussed quality in the dialogues of Plato, where it receives extensive treatment. In the *Phaedrus*, Plato has Socrates provide a list of human types who have most closely been attached to the divine: "but the one that has seen the most [divine] things shall implant in that which will engender a man who will become a philosopher or lover of the beautiful or someone musical and erotic; the second in that of a lawful king or a warlike and commanding one; the third in that of a statesman (*politikos*) or some household manager or businessman."[49] In the *Symposium*, Plato has Socrates claim a "daimonic man" is someone who is wise in "the whole intercourse and conversation of gods with human beings" "for it is in the middle of both and fills up the interval so that the whole itself has been bound together by it."[50] Referring to the *Symposium*, Eric Voegelin describes the "spiritual man, *daimonios aner*, who lives in the tension between needy and full being" and who is supremely erotic, as Eros is "the symbol of the tension experienced between the poles of temporal and eternal being," where the divine and human partake in one another.[51] He is also the measure of right and possesses the "power of influence on others—and the reciprocal experience of gratitude" in others.[52] As we shall see later in this book, Churchill

---

49 Plato, *Phaedrus*, 248d. The remaining nine types are: "lover of gymnastic toil," prophet, poet, craftsman or farmer, sophist, and, finally, tyrant.
50 Plato, *Symposium*, 203a.
51 Eric Voegelin, *Anamnesis*, 325–26.
52 Richard J. Bishirjian, "Daimonic Men," 159.

frequently spoke of the importance of seeing the "whole scene" in order to bring about order. Daimonism is the mark of the "creative prince," for whom *governing is creativity*, an encompassing and incessant process of creation."[53]

More than what Aristotle's notion of magnanimity or "mature man [*spoudaios*]" captures, Plato's notion of the musical or daimonic soul (and Churchill's understanding of Moses) who has partaken of the divine suggests the capacity to understand and love things that truly are, above and beyond the flitting winds of the current moment, the beautiful that uplifts souls from the base and ugly, and the capacity to discern and bring forth greatness in others. The daimonic man has a special sense of his own political actions. As Voegelin states in the context of the Homeric heroes: "Action at the heroic height, thus, is as much human as it is the manifestation of a divine force. And the public order of a society, in so far as at critical junctures it depends on the forthcoming of such action, is precariously maintained in being at the borderline of this meeting of human with divine forces."[54] Indeed, Churchill, despite his professed disbelief in the immortal soul, seems seriously to have taken himself as an amanuensis for divine forces acting in history.[55] This belief was reflected in the divine care he believed saved him in the Boer War and that used him to become the victor in World War Two. His reflection upon becoming Prime Minister is perhaps the most famous of his statements concerning this: "At last I had the authority to give directions over the whole scene. I felt as if I were walking with Destiny, and that all my past life had been but a preparation for this hour and for this trial."[56]

In short, daimonism is a very special capacity for friendship and practical wisdom. The daimonic man is demiurgic. He is the statesman who acts "at the borderline of . . . human and divine forces."

---

53 Tilo Schabert, "A Classical Prince: The Style of François Mitterrand," 235.
54 Voegelin, *World of the Polis*, 104.
55 For discussion with reference to Plato's views on these matters, see my *The Form of Politics*, Chapter 7. See also Paul Addison, "Destiny, History and Providence: The Religion of Winston Churchill," 238–48, and Andrew Roberts, "Winston Churchill and Religion—A Comfortable Relationship with the Almighty."
56 Churchill, *The Second World War*, vol. 1, 601.

Churchill's own daimonism can be seen in his personal eccentricities, his aesthetic sensibilities,[57] his musical speech-making, and, above, all, his capacity to "connect" with others in face-to-face encounters, and in his speeches to large audiences. Indeed, if daimonism involves a fluid "borderline" between oneself and the world (including "divine forces"), this may help to explain his "limpidity" or transparency of character, as well even as his propensity to display his naked body. Waller Newell describes these characteristics as marks of his magnanimity, which they are, but "daimonism" seems better to capture their essence.[58]

Churchill's practical wisdom, his leadership, and his capacity to inspire his countrymen, to touch their inmost hopes and aspirations, through his musical speeches during World War Two, are some of the most pronounced examples of his own daimonism. One reviewer of his wartime speeches claimed: "He not only makes laws for his people but writes their songs as well."[59] Churchill's speeches also follow the rhythms and cadences of the King James Bible. Indeed, in writing out his speeches, he would adopt the "psalm" format of blank verse format with the lines after the first line indented, just as the psalms get published.[60] Churchill also considered it a key attribute of the statesmanship of John Churchill, Duke of Marlborough, whose biography he published in the 1930s. The importance Churchill placed upon Marlborough's daimonism is examined in Chapter Eight.

Moses as Friend and Political Leader

Of the Moses essay, Jonathan Rose observes: "Two themes dominate the essay: the relevance of the Exodus story to contemporary politics, and the author's strong identification with the hero of the piece."[61] Writing

57 See Jonathan Rose, *The Literary Churchill*, chapter 1.
58 Waller Newell, *The Soul of a Leader*, 49.
59 Malcolm Cowley, "Mr. Churchill Speaks," 537.
60 I thank Allen Packwood, director of Churchill Archives at Churchill College, Cambridge University, for this information.
61 Rose, *The Literary Churchill*, 177. Rose's study of Churchill could also be regarded as a study of Churchill's musical soul.

with reference to himself during his own "exile" years, Churchill explains: "Every prophet has to come from civilization, but every prophet has to go into the wilderness. He must have a strong impression of a complex society and all that it has to give, and then he must serve periods of isolation and meditation. This is the process by which psychic dynamite is made."[62]

Churchill discusses how the miracles Moses performed can be explained largely by natural causation:

> The strong north wind which is said to have blown back the waters of the Red Sea may well have been assisted by a seismic and volcanic disturbance. Geologists tell us that the same fault in the earth's structure which cleft the depression of the Dead Sea in Palestine runs unbroken to the Rift Valley . . . . The Sinai peninsula was once volcanic, and the Bible descriptions of Mount Sinai both by day and by night are directly explicable by an eruption, which would have provided at once the pillar of cloud by daylight and of fire in the darkness . . . . All these purely rationalistic and scientific explanations only prove the truth of the Bible story. It is silly wasting time arguing whether Jehovah broke His own natural laws to save His Chosen People, or whether He merely made them work in a favorable manner.[63]

After listing several instances of miracles that are fully explicable according to science, Churchill adds:

> At any rate, there is no doubt about one miracle. This wandering tribe, in many respects indistinguishable from numberless nomadic communities, grasped and proclaimed an

62 Churchill, "Moses, the Leader of a People," in *Thoughts and Adventures*, 304.

63 Churchill, "Moses, the Leader of a People," in *Thoughts and Adventures*, 309. Churchill's view of miracles and natural causation is not as unorthodox as it seems. Augustine provides a similar view in his *Confessions* (see Frederick J. Crosson, "Structure and Meaning in St. Augustine's *Confessions*").

idea of which all the genius of Greece and all the power were incapable. There was to be only one God, a universal God, a God of nations, a just God, a God who would punish in another world a wicked man dying rich and prosperous; a God from whose service the good of the humble and of the weak and poor was inseparable.[64]

This great miracle was predicated upon the miracle that was Moses. Churchill describes of the Burning Bush episode: "[God] said from the Burning Bush, now surely inside the frame of Moses, 'I will endow you with superhuman power. There is nothing that man cannot do, if he wills it with enough resolution. Man is the epitome of the universe. All moves and exists as a result of his invincible will, which is My Will.'"[65] Keeping in mind Churchill's self-narration while writing about Moses, this statement is reminiscent of one he made celebrating his 75th birthday in 1949: "I am ready to meet my Maker. Whether my Maker is prepared for the great ordeal of meeting me is another matter."[66] Churchill too took in the Burning Bush, as seen in what Boris Johnson calls the "Churchill factor."[67] It is seen in Churchill's own resolute will in leading the war effort and reflected in his famous "We Shall Fight on the Beaches" speech as well as in his famous insistence on the importance of hope, expressed when he stated, "Whether you believe or disbelieve, it is a wicked thing to take away Man's hope."[68] This internalized Burning Bush seems equivalent to the more differentiated notion of *daimonios aner* because it points to the miracle of unswerving and seemingly inexhaustible

---

64   Churchill, "Moses, the Leader of a People," in *Thoughts and Adventures*, 309–10.
65   Churchill, "Moses, the Leader of a People," 305. Muller states with some irony in the accompanying footnote that this is a "very broad interpretation of Exodus 4–5." This is true but beside the point because, as with Churchill's other writings, he is engaging in self-revelation and mythopoesis, not interpretation of texts or events.
66   Langworth, *Churchill in His Own Words*, 463.
67   Boris Johnson, *The Churchill Factor*.
68   Meacham, *Franklin and Winston*, 29, citing Anthony Montague Brown, *Long Sunset*, 204.

determination in pursuing great purposes, and the capacities for friendship required to bring along a people toward those purposes.

For Churchill, Moses' sole weakness was that he was not eloquent. He needed a counterpart to give voice to his "driving force": "A competent politician and trained speaker in the shape of one Aaron would be provided. Moses now remembered his kinsman Aaron, with whom he had been good friends before he had to flee from Egypt. Thereupon action!"[69] Thus one of the greatest leaders of people had as his complement and spokesman his "friend." This would have required a great degree of equality between the two, as well as they would have had to enjoy what Aristotle refers to as virtue-friendship, for Aaron would have had to have understood Moses' own mind, and therefore God's will, to a large extent to have been a satisfactory spokesman. It is noteworthy that after Churchill calls Aaron his "kinsman," he refers to Aaron as Moses' "friend," which the King James Bible does not do.[70] Churchill does not explain his modified terminology. Perhaps that Aaron was his kinsman and brother was obvious to him, and it made little difference what he called him. Or perhaps Churchill wished to point to something about their relationship and the aim of that relationship by referring to Aaron as his friend. A brother or kinsman is a natural or biological relationship, whereas friendship is a freer relationship. There is greater freedom, based more on principle than on accident of biology or history, in a friend than in a brother. Friendship is a union of mind and soul, whereby kin relations do not necessarily rise to that level.

Indeed, the aim of their friendship was to open up a space of freedom amidst the forces of natural necessity in order to instantiate an important idea into history, that of the universal God of nations. Great deeds, especially those that found new moral orders based upon universal principles, depend on great leaders who rely on good and loyal friends. Their friends are perhaps not as great as the leaders themselves, but they ably complement those leaders in such a way that make them also great. The two adorn one another. This is what Churchill sought in both

69 Churchill, "Moses, the Leader of a People," 305.
70 Exodus 4:14. Muller points out that Aaron was Moses' brother, as if to correct Churchill (305 n.30).

Beaverbrook and in Roosevelt in his own quest to defend liberty against the Germanic Pharaoh.[71]

Of course Churchill notices that the new order that Moses brought forth surpassed the "genius of Greece and all the power of Rome." Their greatness surpasses even that of Plato or Aristotle, to whom we have drawn comparisons. In his "Flame of Christian Ethics" address to the University of Oslo, he states in this spirit: "The Greek and Latin philosophers often seem to have been unaware that the society in which they lived was founded upon slavery. They spoke of freedom and political institutions, but they were quite unaware that their culture was built upon quite detestable foundations."[72] It is noteworthy that in that later address he chose the daimonic "flame" to describe the motivational core of Christian ethics.

Even so, the moral and political order Moses, with Aaron, established impressed Churchill. He states in *The Second World War* that:

> The [since Christianized] Greeks rival the Jews in being the most politically-minded race in the world. No matter how forlorn their circumstances or how grave the peril to their country, they are always divided into many parties. . . . No two races have set such a mark upon the world. Both have shown a capacity for survival, in spite of unending perils and sufferings from external oppressors, matched only by their own ceaseless feuds, quarrels, and convulsions. . . . No two cities have counted more with mankind than Athens and Jerusalem. Their messages in religion, philosophy, and art have been the main guiding lights of modern faith and culture. . . . Personally I have always been on the side of both, and believed in their invincible power to survive internal strife and the world tides threatening their extinction.[73]

71 Rose finds numerous literary precedents for Churchill's political actions in his own writings as well as in the writings of others. Rose notes how *Savrola*, Churchill's early novel, is an anti-fascist tract that played out forty years after it was published. The "Moses" essay also provides a similar plot for Churchillian politics (*The Literary Churchill*, 72, 177–79).
72 Churchill, "The Flame of Christian Ethics," 7646.
73 Churchill, *The Second World War*, vol. 5, 470–01.

For Churchill, Moses's friendship with Aaron established a robust political order based upon freedom and friendship (or covenant, in this case) that is also the main cause for its perseverance amidst centuries of convulsions. The basis upon which the Jews (and Greeks) founded their civilizations transcended those tides and gave them their resilience.

Israel was followed by the revelation of Christ, who revealed God as God "not only of Israel, but of all mankind who wished to serve Him; a God not only of justice, but of mercy; a God not only of self-preservation and survival, but of pity, self-sacrifice, and ineffable love."[74] Churchill's practice of friendship in politics extended as far as singing England's "island story," and beyond that, the British Empire and, beyond even that, the "English-speaking peoples." It enabled him to care for the good of Germans after their defeat, having been overcome with compassion for "haggard" bombed-out Berliners during a tour of the city at the Potsdam conference.[75] However, it also led him to be careless, if not malevolent, toward India, to which, for one, he was never willing to concede independence and which suffered a horrific famine during World War Two.[76] Even so, Churchill realized political friendship is lower than the universal love commanded by Jesus Christ. It is also bound geographically and culturally, in contrast to the mystical body of the Church, "all mankind who wished to serve Him." The Sermon on the Mount is the highest ethic, but it is not, as we saw, for politicians. According to Colville: "The PM said their greatness [of religious leaders] was indisputable but it was of a different kind. Christ's story was unequalled and his death to save sinners unsurpassed; moreover the Sermon on the

---

74 Churchill, "Moses, the Leader of a People," 311.

75 Stelzer, *Dinner With Churchill*, 221.

76 On empire, see Emmert, *Winston S. Churchill on Empire* and James, *Churchill and Empire*. On the famine in India, see James, *Churchill and Empire*, 303–6 and Richard Toye, *Churchill's Empire*, 234–40. Larry Arnn argues the Japanese blockade of India caused the famine and, if anything, Churchill prevented the famine from being worse than it was (*Churchill's Trial: Winston Churchill and the Salvation of Free Government*, 97–116). In Chapter Six, I consider the tension produced by empire in Churchill's view of politics.

Mount was the last word in ethics."[77] It seems Christian ethics is uniquely qualified to help us understand and perhaps to effect justice. Considering again his "Flame of Christian Ethics" speech: "The flame of Christian ethics is still our best guide. Its animation and accomplishment is a practical necessity, both spiritually and materially. This is the most vital question of the future. The accomplishment of Christian ethics in our daily life is the final and greatest word which has ever been said. Only on this basis can we reconcile the rights of the individual with the demands of society in a manner which alone can bring happiness and peace to humanity."[78]

If Churchill drew further lessons from the friendship of Moses and Aaron, he does not indicate them in the essay. The essay is pivotal for understanding the larger picture of Churchill's views. For instance, Rose observes that the Exodus story, which held such personal appeal to his style of leading a nation against all odds, also became the foundation of his passionate Zionism; indeed he later exhorted the leaders of the newly formed state of Israel to "preserve close association with the book."[79] The other aspects of the Moses and Aaron friendship do not seem to have caught his attention, nor do they really fit his friendships with Beaverbrook or, as we shall see, Roosevelt. These other aspects include Aaron's voicing the views and passions of the Israelites that lead both to their falling away from their mission (i.e., worshipping the Golden Calf) and to the construction of the tabernacle. According to Aaron Wildavsky, Aaron needfully represents the people in their everyday existence, a necessary respite from the energy and exhortation they received from Moses: "The people cannot continually live at an exalted level; every day cannot be a holy day . . . . Just as the people need a Moses for great occasions, they need an Aaron for the time in between."[80]

However, Wildavsky's summary of the complementarity between Moses and Aaron illuminates something that may have been missing in

77   Colville, *Fringes of Power*, 648. See Grant Havers, *Leo Strauss and American Democracy*, 106.

78   Churchill, "The Flame of Christian Ethics," 7645.

79   Rose, *The Literary Churchill*, 180.

80   Aaron Wildavsky, *Moses as Political Leader*, 125.

Churchill's friendships. For Churchill and his sense of adventure, it could be said all days are at the "exalted level"; there is no "time in between," especially during World War Two when he promised the people "I have nothing to offer but blood, toil, tears and sweat." This was especially evident when Churchill (and Beaverbrook) misread the public mood that led to his loss in the 1945 election. He simply was not interested in the people's genuine yearning for material security and comfort, which gave the election to the Socialists who obviously understood this of the British people. Churchill and his friends, perhaps precisely because they, in Jenkins' description of them as outsiders with a "touch of loucheness,"[81] were simply incapable of living in the "time in between."

Even so, Churchill could also combine the virtues both of Moses, as leader, and Aaron, as representative of the people, which can be seen in his capacity to sustain during the war an emotional and intellectual connection with the British people that inspired and comforted them. It seems his musical and daimonic sense of melodrama and tragedy appealed to their inmost sense of themselves.[82] The main lesson from Moses that Churchill drew for himself was how great political leaders depend on complementary friends.

We turn in the next chapter to his practice of friendships in politics, first with Max Aitken (Lord Beaverbrook) and then, on a larger stage, Franklin Roosevelt.

---

81 Jenkins, *Churchill: A Biography*, 648.
82 Rose, *The Literary Churchill*, 331.

Part Two
Friends With Statesmen

Chapter Three
Lord Beaverbrook, "Foul Weather" Friend

Magnanimous Friends

Churchill and Max Aitken, or Lord Beaverbrook, first met in 1910 and solidified their friendship in 1915 when Churchill led the Admiralty and Beaverbrook was also a member of Lloyd George's government. Beaverbrook, a Canadian, played a role in the downfall of Prime Minister Asquith and the elevation of Lloyd George in 1916, and his role as backroom intriguer was well-known for years after. He became Lord Beaverbrook when he received his peerage in 1917. He was appointed Minister of Information in 1918, owing in part to his vast holdings of English newspapers. They continued their friendship during the 1920s but had little to do with one another during Churchill's "exile" years in the 1930s, although by 1937 Beaverbrook's *Evening Standard* "had become the main outlet" for Churchill's newspaper articles.[1] Beaverbrook supported Chamberlain's policies toward Germany, even supporting making a separate peace with Hitler after the invasion of France, and thought Churchill too much of a war-monger.[2] At Beaverbrook's initiative, their friendship resumed in 1940.

In May 1940, Beaverbrook joined the War Cabinet as Minister of Aircraft Production. After quitting in April 1941 (and again in February 1942 as Minister of War Production) due to exhaustion, Churchill appointed him Minister without portfolio, and then as Lord Privy Seal in September 1943. At least until the fall of Tobruk in June 1942,

1   Jenkins, *Churchill: A Biography*, 506.
2   Their divergent foreign policy views led to the termination of Churchill's contract with the *Evening Standard* (Jenkins, *Churchill: A Biography*, 516).

Beaverbrook was perhaps Churchill's most dangerous Cabinet minister because of his apparent (and delusional) ambition to succeed Churchill as Prime Minister. During this time, he used his position as press baron to advocate positions contrary to government policy, especially to open a second front to assist the Soviet Union.[3]

Even so, there was something more than sheer political considerations that sustained their relationship during this time. Bercuson and Herwig claim of Beaverbrook: "It was said that he was the only man in English public life who could truly match wits with Churchill. He was a major influence on key political questions confronting Britain in the decade before the outbreak of the war, and in that decade he was more often opposed to Churchill than in agreement with him."[4] It seems Churchill simply wanted him around because by then the two had cemented their close friendship. They were the only men who served in Cabinet during both World Wars, and Beaverbrook was the only one to serve in Churchill's Cabinet without a portfolio. Churchill's general rule was that political power must be yoked to political responsibility, but he made an exception for the contradictory Beaverbrook. One reason was that he needed Beaverbrook's considerable talents. He frequently served as Churchill's personal emissary to foreign heads of state, including Stalin, with whom he had tremendous rapport. Schneer argues Beaverbrook's greatest achievement during the war was not as Minister of Aircraft Production, but in persuading the Americans to increase their production targets.[5] But Churchill also wanted Beaverbrook around simply because they were good friends. He wanted Beaverbrook's counsel and his "buoyancy." He was one of the few he could trust completely. Indeed, Beaverbrook's influence (and that of Brendan Bracken) was a

3   Jonathan Schneer describes their tumultuous political friendship, amidst their long-standing personal friendship, during World War Two while Beaverbrook served in Cabinet (*Ministers at War: Winston Churchill and His War Cabinet*, 155–78). Of all the Cabinet ministers, Schneer claims Beaverbrook "represented the greatest danger" to Churchill's position. The fall of Tobruk took the wind out of Beaverbrook's argument for a second front, and thus his hopes to be successor.

4   David Bercuson and Holger Herwig, *One Christmas in Washington*, 103.

5   Schneer, *Ministers at War: Winston Churchill and His War Cabinet*, 165.

source of discontent among other members of Cabinet, who thought he exercised undue influence on Churchill.[6] Beaverbrook was widely distrusted for many of the same reasons Churchill was: he was supremely ambitious and talented, but many questioned his judgment. Beaverbrook described his own ethos: "I am not a committee man. I am the cat that walks alone."[7] To understand their friendship is to understand the challenges of practicing friendship with cats that walk alone.

Their friendship was a political alliance that helped Great Britain during the war, but they also saw their friendship in a greater moral light that transcended the game of politics. In many ways, they shared the kind of friendship that Aristotle calls *sunaisthesis* that is the very characteristic of human life: "this would come through living together and sharing conversation and thinking; for this would seem to be what living together means in the case of human beings."[8]

Magnanimity and daimonism, the two categories we saw in the last chapter that appealed to Churchill's understanding of political greatness, inform his friendship with Max Aitken, or Lord Beaverbrook. What follows is less a summary of their friendship than an explanation of their bond in these terms.[9] Indeed, these are the terms their contemporaries used to describe the two men's enigmatic friendship.

Harry Hopkins, Franklin Roosevelt's good friend and closest advisor, described the friendship of Churchill and Beaverbrook:

> Here were two determined and inherently powerful men whose very similarities clashed; both were supreme patriots on an imperial scale, both were tireless and tenacious, both extremely worldly, with great zest and capacity for good living, both were superb showmen with an alert ability for spotting and appreciating the main chance; and each of the many disagreements between them seemed utterly irreconcilable

---

6   Jenkins, *Churchill: A Biography*, 774.
7   Beaverbrook to Churchill, January 3, 1941, quoted by Jonathan Schneer, *Ministers at War: Winston Churchill and His War Cabinet*, 157.
8   Aristotle, *Nicomachean Ethics*, 1170b10–13.
9   For their friendship, see Kenneth Young, *Churchill and Beaverbrook* and A. J. P. Taylor, *Beaverbrook*.

until a common contempt for the purely transient issue brought them together again.[10]

Hopkins described their friendship as one shared by two public-minded and spirited men whose crackling personalities made it surprising the two actually got along so well. To use a moral term that both Churchill and Beaverbrook liked to describe of themselves and of one another, they were two magnanimous men, for they shared "a common contempt for the purely transient issue" (usually domestic policy matters). As explained in the previous chapter, magnanimous men make few friends, but when they do it is intense. Thus, Churchill's two great political friendships, with Beaverbrook (examined in this chapter) and with Roosevelt (examined in Chapters Four and Five), were exceedingly rare instances of "sunaisthetic" friendship between magnanimous men.

As noted in the previous chapter, Aristotle thought the magnanimous man has a conflicted soul. He seeks honours as the greatest external good, but he also seeks genuine honours. He seeks honours and he seeks truth, and these two aspirations do not always align. The conflicted soul of the magnanimous man perhaps explains why so many of Churchill's and Beaverbrook's contemporaries regarded them both as contradictory. Consider the judgment of General Ismay, Churchill's chief military assistant during World War Two: "You cannot judge the Prime Minister by ordinary standards . . . . He is not in the least like anyone that you or I have ever met. He is a mass of contradictions . . . : either in an angelic temper or a hell of a rage: when he isn't fast asleep he's a volcano. There are no half-measures in his make-up. He is a child of nature with moods as variable as an April day."[11] Ismay has in mind the impatience Churchill would on occasion display toward staffers. However, given what was at stake for Churchill's leadership and the pressures that were placed upon him, his impatience is understandable. There are no "half-measures" for

---

10 Kenneth Young, *Churchill and Beaverbrook*, quoted 254.
11 Quoted in Dilks, *Churchill and Company*, 158. Ismay's claim regarding Churchill's "mass of contradictions" is the governing metaphor of his book. This accords with Beaverbrook's assessment that there is "Churchill Up" and "Churchill Down."

someone striving to achieve, in Aristotelian terms, "great things" and his "hell of a rage" can generally be attributed to the failures of himself and those he commanded to become "worthy" of those objectives.

The judgment of John Colville, Churchill's secretary, of Beaverbrook having a contradictory nature expresses a similar judgment:

> The thesis is a man of superhuman drive, of ingenuity and imagination, of generosity to friends and adversaries alike, especially when they were in distress or in disgrace, and a zealous champion of the unorthodox. The antithesis is a juggler with men and money, an incorrigible intriguer, a prodigious liar, a dedicated mischief-maker and a politician of unsound judgment. The synthesis is Lord Beaverbrook.[12]

The thesis, Beaverbrook's "superhuman drive," could be seen in his prodigious success as a businessman and the tremendous effort he exerted as Minister of Aircraft Production, which proved so pivotal for England during the first part of World War Two. His "generosity to friends and adversaries . . . when they were in distress or disgrace" was reflected in his habit of being a "foul-weather friend" for numerous individuals in Britain's political class, including Bonar Law and Churchill, not to mention Canadian Prime Minister R. B. Bennett, the subject of Beaverbrook's book, *Friends*.[13] As Beaverbrook's biographer and friend, A. J. P. Taylor argues, "Nothing was deeper or more constant in him than to be a foul-weather friend. Many spurned him when they were Up and yet received consolation from him when they were Down."[14] Taylor's reference to "Up" and "Down" refers to Beaverbrook's own description of "Churchill Up" and "Churchill Down," first made apparently when Churchill was "Down" after Bonar Law excluded him from the Admiralty.

The antithesis, Beaverbrook's juggling with "men and money, an incorrigible intriguer," reflects his role as kingmaker or puppet-player of

---

12   John Colville, *Winston Churchill and His Inner Circle*, 88.
13   Beaverbrook, *Friends: Sixty Years of Intimate Personal Relations with Richard Bedford Bennett*.
14   A. J. P. Taylor, *Beaverbrook*, 95.

British politics between the two wars, which also includes his own role, it seems, in keeping Churchill out of politics in the early twenties and again during the "exile years" in the 1930s.[15] His prodigious lying and mischief-making was seen most clearly during his time as Minister of Aircraft Production when he used many dubious if not illegal means to obtain materials for production. This included stealing parts from other factories in England as well as commandeering aircraft to fly to France to pick up loads of damaged engines and components for use in repair factories in England, and organizing militias to guard supplies, even supplying them with small armoured cars, called Beaverettes and Beaverbugs.[16] While Colville posits Beaverbrook as the synthesis, he lets it be known that, as with Ismay's assessment of Churchill, Beaverbrook was a "mass of contradictions." The friendship of these two masses of contradictions can best be understood in terms of the magnanimous man's conflicted soul, who indeed seems arrogant and haughty to those who are not magnanimous or to those who cannot keep up with his own march through the desert.

From the first time they met, each recognized the greatness, or at least aspiration to greatness, of the other. Despite or because of Beaverbrook's stormy personality as an intriguer, Churchill trusted him. And herein lies the key paradox of their friendship, which was famous for its conflicts, flare-ups, and fights, which at one point led the Secretary of Cabinet to remark to King George VI's secretary: "They abused each other like a pair of fishwives."[17]

We saw in the last chapter how the death of F. E. Smith hit Churchill hard, and how crucial friends, like Moses and Aaron, are for helping and complementing one another. We shall see this again in Chapters Eight and Nine when we consider Churchill's treatment of Marlborough and Eugene of Savoy. Great leaders need to recognize their deficiencies and their need for friendship. More than that, perhaps, they prize sharing the exuberant joy of adventure with a friend. Indeed, Beaverbrook

---

15   Young, *Churchill and Beaverbrook*, 62, 73.
16   Young, *Churchill and Beaverbrook*, 157. See also David Adams Richard, *Lord Beaverbrook*, 141–50.
17   Dilks, *Churchill and Company: Allies and Rivals in War and Peace*, 53.

drew a similar conclusion when he argued that what made Churchill a better war leader than Lloyd George was Churchill's capacity for friendship, a capacity that enabled him to make "cruel and heartrending" decisions (including Churchill's decision to sink the French fleet in Oran, on which Beaverbrook counseled him). Great leaders with capacity for friendship enjoy the loyalty of their friends, as well as their counsel and succor.[18]

Beaverbrook and Churchill's Shared Daimonism

In his study of Churchill and Beaverbrook, Kenneth Young claims that something like what we have identified as the Burning Bush or adornment (*kosmos*) was present in attracting the two men to one another:

> The two men had met in 1910; they became intimates during the First World War, colleagues and cronies in the Second; and they died within a few months of each other in 1964–65, having known each other for fifty-five years. In many ways totally unlike, they had one thing in common: a spark of divine energy which each recognized in the other.[19]

They each seemed to have possessed something of the daimonic, which Socrates claims statesmen must have.[20] This "spark of divine energy" is enigmatic:

> [Churchill] was a man cut out of no common mould. Aristocrat was inadequate to describe him. So were professional soldier, journalist or even senior minister of the Crown. He was at once all and more; and Aitken, himself no mere New

---

18 Beaverbrook, "Two War Leaders," 551–52. Andrew Roberts evaluates this essay and finds "most of Beaverbrook's evaluations have stood the test of time; it is the facts on which he based them that today look faulty" ("The Goat and the Bulldog," 72).

19 Young, *Churchill and Beaverbrook*, 11–12.

20 Plato, *Phaedrus*, 248d.

World millionaire, was drawn to him as the iron filing to the lodestone.[21]

According to Young, there was something indefinable, beyond words or perhaps reason, about their friendship that enabled it to withstand numerous "rows" and arguments:

> Friendship does not, of course, depend on perfect agreement all the time; many friendships are founded on disagreement. But there must be a liking, that indefinable *sympathie*, which is much more decisive than coincidence of interests or similar tastes and backgrounds. *Sympathie* there was between Churchill and Beaverbrook from the beginning—or at any rate a complete absence of that bristling as much a feature of human relationships as of dogs. On the face of it, this is surprising. Both were strong men accustomed to having their own way; both were men of power, political power in the one case, money power in the other, and to neither had it come easily: "We both had big jobs to do when we were young," Aitken wrote to Churchill thirty years later; and he wrote of Churchill that he was impetuous, determined and not always judicious. The words applied no less to Aitken. "Like Churchill," he wrote, "I was arrogant in my young years." Similarities of this kind usually lead to collision not to friendship. In other ways they were complete opposites— to such a degree that it might be supposed that they could scarcely make contact with each other.[22]

Young pinpoints something crucial by describing their friendship in terms of "liking, that indefinable *sympathie*," indicating several times

21 Young, *Churchill and Beaverbrook*, 24. Boris Johnson speaks of the "Churchill factor" when explaining his characteristic greatness that eludes categorization (*The Churchill Factor*). Young's reference to friendship-love as a lodestone is the same as that which Plato in the *Laws* uses to describe the attraction of the Magnesians to one another and to Nous in the best practical regime (Plato, *Laws* 666c).
22 Young, *Churchill and Beaverbrook*, 25.

that neither could really provide an account of what they saw in the other that made them friends. Elizabeth Telfer describes the activity of "liking" in similar terms:

> The degree of rationality which this involves, however, is rather limited. For even where we can give our reasons for liking someone or feeling a bond with him, we cannot further justify these reasons . . . . And we may find it very difficult to state our reasons at all. In such a case the most we might be prepared to say is that there must be qualities in the friend, even if we cannot "pin them down". . . . Liking is a difficult phenomenon to analyze . . . . It seems rather to be a quasi-aesthetic attitude, roughly specifiable as "finding a person to one's taste" . . . . In reality our reaction, like a reaction to a picture, is to a whole personality seen as a unified thing. This is why we often find it very difficult to say what it is we like about a person. Sometimes what we like is partly the way in which everything about the person seems to "hang together" and be part of a unified style; sometimes we enjoy a contrast, for example that between a mild unassuming exterior and an iron determination.[23]

Young suggests Aitken was attracted to Churchill's ambition and desire for glory. Beaverbrook initially saw great but unformed talent in the younger Churchill in 1915 and in the 1920s, where he "was first 'dazzled' by Churchill's brilliant powers."[24] At that time he determined that for all his energy Churchill lacked maturity and judgment. By 1940 he realized that Churchill fully formed was indeed a magnanimous statesman. They both seemed to be attracted to the "buccaneering" element in the other. Indeed, Young observes that all of Churchill's small group of friends like Smith, Bracken, and Beaverbrook were "originals," and for this reason were distrusted by Churchill's wife, Clementine. Churchill was said to have remarked on occasion that "Some people take drugs; I

23 Elizabeth Telfer, "Friendship," 253.
24 Young, *Churchill and Beaverbrook*, 24.

take Max."[25] He was Churchill's "principal stimulant and mentor" and appreciated Beaverbrook's "personal buoyancy and vigor" to the extent that he could not conceive of his War Cabinet without Beaverbrook, more because of his buoyancy than even his considerable competency.[26] Churchill simply needed Beaverbrook, the "foul weather friend," to lift him up and for his counsel.

Young gets quite close to equating Churchill's desire for glory with the Aristotelian version: "His 'gleam' was more in tune with Dante's than with Joseph Chamberlain's. It was a vision beyond the imagining of Aitken. Probably this was the mysterious 'x' which intrigued Aitken from the time he first met Churchill and which he never entirely explained to himself."[27] Young chooses a religious and political image to describe the root of the attraction. Ancient cultures frequently portrayed great leaders with a halo, and premodern political thinkers like Plato, Aristotle, Augustine, Aquinas, and Dante explicitly associate *clara* or *gloria* with images of light. The glorified statesmen literally shines out, which expresses Churchill's ambition quite very well.[28]

Yet this glory or "central fire" is paradoxical and enigmatic because the glorified, like the magnanimous man, also stands apart and alone. Churchill knew this, as expressed in his favorite quatrain on greatness, taken from Henry Wadsworth Longfellow's "Ladder of St. Augustine": "The heights by great men reached and kept/ Were not attained by sudden flight/ But they while their companions slept/ Were toiling upwards through the night," which Beaverbrook could quote back to Churchill in a moment of shared understanding.[29]

Though the gloried or magnanimous man is a loner to a degree, his desire for greatness can make his friendships stronger because they are

25 Dilks, *Churchill and Company*, 45. See Young, *Churchill and Beaverbrook*, 12.

26 Young, *Churchill and Beaverbrook*, 64, 155, 183.

27 Ibid., 28.

28 Augustine defines glory "clear knowledge together with praise" (*clara cum laude notitia*). For details, see my *Augustine and Politics as Longing in the World*, 150–71.

29 Young, *Churchill and Beaverbrook*, 95. Churchill apparently did not know the authorship of the quatrain, though Beaverbrook did know.

so rare. Young explains: "But when—after years of acquaintance—he did make a friend outside the charmed circle he cherished him with the same indulgence and defended him, right or wrong, with the same doggedness as if he were a member of his own family . . . . But the friendship once made persisted despite differences of opinion, of politics, or of taste."[30] Friendship slow to be won, in such cases, is as permanent as permanent can be. Indeed, Beaverbrook once wrote that, "I do not know a fault in his life, save only too strong a devotion to his friends."[31]

Beaverbrook and Churchill's friendship withstood numerous shocks but yet endured. Perhaps the most significant instance of their tumultuous friendships—we have noted their frequent spirited arguments—is the fact that Churchill tolerated Beaverbrook's frequent threats to resign as Minister of Aircraft Production. Churchill seemed to understand that Beaverbrook's frequent threats to resign was a strategy, "a deliberate act of promotion. The object was 'urgency and speed'" to pressure other departments to lend support to his efforts.[32] For Churchill generally, a Minister resigning during wartime was equivalent to treachery. Churchill once told him: "You are in the galleys and will have to row to the end."[33] In 1942 Churchill told him "People don't resign in war; you either die or are sacked."[34] Yet Churchill finally allowed him to resign from that position, only to bring him back by his side, first in Cabinet as Minister without portfolio and then outside as Lord Privy Seal, just so he could have him around for his counsel and competence in performing high-level tasks and, more importantly, for his good company and friendship. According to Colville, Churchill regarded Beaverbrook among those, if not first among those, with whom "it is agreeable to dine."[35] For these reasons, Beaverbrook was Churchill's friend and confidante during the war. As Young argues, "Often Churchill took his friend into his deepest

---

30 Ibid., 11.
31 Beaverbrook, letter to W. R. Inge, Dean of St. Paul's, cited by Young, *Churchill and Beaverbrook*, 233.
32 Beaverbrook to Churchill, March 17, 1942, quoted by Schneer, *Ministers at War*, 157.
33 Young, *Churchill and Beaverbrook*, 169.
34 Roberts, *Masters and Commanders*, 472.
35 Colville, *Winston Churchill and His Inner Circle*, 97.

confidence and told him his innermost thoughts on the war situation"; he was the chief of Churchill's friends with whom he could discuss matters in the early hours of the morning.[36]

Story-Tellers

They simply liked each other's company. They found each other wonderful conversationalists who recognized each other's greatness which complemented the other's weaknesses. Conversation and story-telling seems key. We saw above that their conversations frequently revolved around their recollections of past glories, and that they shared drafts of their books and even rewrote portions of the other's works. As much as they enjoyed their shared life of action, they seem to have received greater satisfaction from their shared intellectual activity. Sir Robert H. Bruce Lockhart explained: "Apart from the emotionalism and buccaneering spirit which is common to both, those who know the two men best will readily agree that it is the agile brain in Beaverbrook which appeals to Churchill to which the Englishman likes to use as a whetstone on which to sharpen his own remarkable wits."[37] Of this, Beaverbrook seemed to serve as a suitable replacement for F. E. Smith. As with Young's observation that their friendship consisted less in their shared agreement in things human and divine and more in their "liking" of one another, Lockhart suggests that their shared intellectual activity is key to understanding their friendship.

Perhaps nothing illustrates their "sunaisthesis" better than their practice, begun in 1926, of sharing with each other book manuscripts on which each was working. Young claims Churchill's sharing the proofs of the third volume of *The World Crisis* then brought the two "into real intimacy.[38] Young argues theirs "was one of the most interesting collaborations in literary history—and, as we have seen, it was sometimes the cement of friendship when little else could keep them together."[39] Not only did they share proofs

---

36   Young, *Churchill and Beaverbrook*, 154, 186.
37   Quoted in Young, *Churchill and Beaverbrook*, 232.
38   Young, *Churchill and Beaverbrook*, 87.
39   Ibid., 95.

of their books for comment, but each invited the other to rewrite portions if his memory of specific events and figures was better than the other's. For example, Churchill invited Beaverbrook to alter passages dealing with Bonar Law and Kitchener in *The World Crisis*. By the spring of 1927, they had gotten into the habit of exchanging proofs, including by then the first three chapters of Beaverbrook's *Political History of the War, 1914–1916* (later published as *Politicians and the War*). Young comments: "It had now become a habit for the two friends to exchange their proofs not merely so that the one would not be quoting the other in a form which was displeasing or incorrect, but also for each to add his moiety to the work in hand."[40] Their story-telling was to some degree a work of common authorship. Even so, their "moiety" still enabled them to express differences of opinion. As Beaverbrook wrote, let Churchill "take the rough with the smooth." Like their friendship, their authorial "moiety" involved having, in Aristotle's terms, "their rough edges knocked off." [41]

It is significant that their shared story extended as well to sharing proofs of books that did not involve one another, as in the case when Churchill shared the proofs of his *My Early Life*:

> In mid-September [1930] Churchill sent Beaverbrook the proofs of his autobiographical book, *My Early Life*, not in this case because it overlapped their relationship, for it ended when Churchill was still in his early twenties. Churchill wrote, comparing their early years, that "we both had to try very hard when we were young"; and replying Beaverbrook said: "We both had a big job on when we were young. But we have a bigger one now that we are old." In other words, looking back is all very well but the struggle is not over.[42]

This gesture is significant because it confirms that each regarded the other as having an intimate part in his life's story. There is a passage in

40 Ibid.
41 Aristotle, *Nicomachean Ethics*, 1172a17.
42 Young, *Churchill and Beaverbrook*, 113. See also Taylor, *Beaverbrook*, 593.

Thomas Mann's magisterial novel, *Joseph and His Brothers*, where he has Joseph tell his friend: "Literature is a great thing. But greater still, to be sure, is when the life one lives is a story—and that we are in a story together, a most excellent one at that, I am more and more convinced with time. You, however, are part of it because I took you into my story."[43] The life of friends *is* a story, and gets expressed *as* a story. This exchange of proofs and letters is significant because the two seem to acknowledge their shared story extends beyond their initial meeting of one another. They acknowledge they are cut from the same cloth because they have a common background. They also acknowledge their shared story is not complete, for "the struggle is not over." Their souls are knotted together in a common life, considering themselves "worthy of great things, and [being] worthy of them,"[44] as well as telling the stories about them.

Beaverbrook joked that if he could not influence Churchill's politics, perhaps at least he could shape his history. Though meant as a joke, this is no mean task because each regarded the writing of history—their history—as more important than politics. Beaverbrook, a newspaper baron, admired Churchill's journalism. It was brilliant and his writing was stellar and eloquent. Journalism is meant as a truth-telling vocation and forms opinion and, as history, forms the like-mindedness of a political society. Both shared the view that political actions are not complete until accurately and vividly spoken about. Churchill, who seemed to write memos during the war for the sole purpose of using them for his book on World War Two which he had planned out as early as December 1940, exemplifies a view that politics *is* story-telling.[45] Beaverbrook's view was much the same. Colville explains:

> Beaverbrook enjoyed storytelling, an art in which he excelled. I remembered that in January 1944 I had stood with him and Clementine Churchill in the Medina at Marrakech. We had watched dancers, the snake charmers and above all the

---

43 Thomas Mann, *Joseph and His Brothers*, 1233.
44 Aristotle, *Nicomachean Ethics*, 1123b4.
45 This is the argument of Rose, *The Literary Churchill*. On Churchill's planning of *The Second World War*, see ibid., 277.

storytellers who stood surrounded by a crowd of squatting listeners. What they said was unintelligible to us, but their eloquence and the gesticulations fascinated Beaverbrook. He said that storytelling was the same the whole world over and it was a great art to practice.[46]

For all of Beaverbrook's admiration for Churchill as politician and statesman, he, a great press baron, seemed to have most admired Churchill's writing, his story-telling. Other statesmen including Lloyd George were also highly intelligent, but only Churchill had the virtues of a great orator who was capable of speaking the truth in a lively and earnest manner connected with his audience.[47] Churchill unified thought and action, with a little more weight given to the side of thought that was expressed less in him being a philosopher than in him being a pre-eminent conversationalist, story-teller, and historian. We shall elaborate Churchill's storytelling when we consider some of his historical writings, and his Marlborough biography in particular.

That each could "add his moiety to the work in hand" was a sign of their common vision of the good, their *sunaisthesis*.

The Last Chapter

The two friends spent many of their days together after the war, mostly at Beaverbrook's "La Capponcina" residence in the south of France, and leading up to their deaths. They recollected and shared stories and they even debated philosophy and theology. Beaverbrook prepared a book titled *The Divine Propagandist*, which set out his belief that the Incarnation promises personal immortality. It also set out his argument that immortality is necessary because the Providence of God bestowed instincts on its creatures that necessarily do not go to waste. For his part, Churchill told him he wished to die in his sleep and that would be the end.[48] Both views are characteristic of political men such as these two;

---

46 Colville, *Winston Churchill and His Inner Circle*, 95.
47 Young, *Churchill and Beaverbrook*, 94.
48 Ibid., 314.

they are consistent with their magnanimity and the Burning Bush or *kosmos* burning within: one considers it illogical for such a Bush to be extinguished, while the other, whose Bush burnt brighter and hotter than perhaps anyone else in the twentieth century, has had enough.

They also played like little boys. Beaverbrook, who suffered from asthma, had had an electric chair-lift installed on the long staircase of "La Capponcina." But when Churchill visited it was Churchill who used it and Beaverbrook who climbed the stairs because he, five years younger than the 85-year-old Churchill, wanted to show off his youth. Though competitive, it also offered the opportunity for shared enjoyment: "But at every few steps Churchill stopped the lift for his host to catch up and both of them chuckled at their little race."[49]

The two men simply enjoyed each other's company, and many observers noticed an "unspoken sympathy" when they shared their company. Beaverbrook died June 9, 1964. When Churchill's secretary, Anthony Montague-Brown, broke the news to him, "Churchill made no reply but his chin sank on his chest. A great depression settled upon the house."[50] Beaverbrook gone, he was "Churchill Down." Churchill passed away, at age 90, 220 days later.

49   Ibid., 316.
50   Ibid., 326.

Chapter Four
Churchill and Roosevelt
at the Summit of Power

In the final volume of *The Second World War*, Churchill states that Roosevelt "died at the supreme climax of the war, and at the moment when his authority was most needed to guide the policy of the United States."[1] The subtitle of that volume is "Triumph and Tragedy," with tragedy denoting the fact that the "Grand Alliance has failed so far to bring general peace to our anxious world."[2] Churchill's speech to Parliament on April 17, 1945, is a paean to his friendship with the "great man." There he provides a short history of their friendship, including their extensive correspondence, their meetings at Argentia, Washington, Casablanca, Teheran, Quebec, and Yalta, "comprising in all about 120 days of close personal contact."[3] He devotes a full paragraph in his speech praising Roosevelt's fortitude toward his "physical affliction," the paralysis Roosevelt had from polio, and his "extraordinary effort of the spirit over the flesh, of will-power over physical infirmity." This was a sign of his daimonic character that could provide him with the grand vision and leadership of world statesman.[4] Thus concluded Churchill's love and admiration of Roosevelt's greatness that originated at least in 1934, when Churchill published an essay on Roosevelt where he praised as well his statesmanlike qualities, seen in his exercise of dictatorial powers "veiled by constitutional forms."[5]

---

1   Churchill, *The Second World War*, vol. 6, 412.
2   Ibid., "Preface."
3   Ibid., vol. 6, 414.
4   Ibid., vol. 6, 414–15.
5   "Roosevelt From Afar," in *Great Contemporaries*, 359–68. On Churchill's assessment (with reference to Napoleon) of his own "undefined" and "very

Surprisingly, Churchill chose not to attend Roosevelt's funeral, even though he had the opportunity to do so, and where he could have met Harry S. Truman. Some, like Roy Jenkins, view his choice not to attend as a sign that Churchill, despite appearances, did not consider Roosevelt his friend: "It was more a partnership of circumstance and convenience than a friendship of individuals, each of whom . . . was a star of brightness which needed its own unimpeded orbit."[6] Jenkins' biography skips over much of Churchill's personal relationship with Roosevelt, focusing instead on his friendship with Harry Hopkins whom he regards as Churchill's "real friend" and with whom he was far more at ease.[7] However, it is difficult to judge Jenkins' assessment as he does not dwell much on any other evidence. More convincing is Jon Meacham's judgment, in his focused study of their friendship, that Churchill's decision not to attend Roosevelt's funeral was a "fit of pride." Having been the wooer of Roosevelt and the United States, Churchill at the end of the war wanted Truman, the junior partner, to come to him.[8] Indeed, if their relationship had been nothing other than "raw politics," Churchill would have gone without hesitation. Churchill's friendship with Roosevelt must be understood within the context of the tough game of statesmanship that each great-souled man played. That is the best way to understand the tensions that characterize their friendship, which those of us who are not statesmen regard with some perplexity.

These men shared what Churchill, in his Marlborough biography, calls the "highest outlook of the war," which was made possible by each

---

wide powers," offered by the "short and obscure" British constitution that required "no legal or constitutional change," see *The Second World War*, vol. 2, 15–16.

6   Jenkins, *Churchill: A Biography*, 785. Jenkins bases his view on the assumption that "great stars are only happy in their own unimpeded orbits" (671). His analytical framework is also that of Churchill's magnanimity, but he differs from mine by concluding that such men, Churchill included, do not generally practice friendship, least of all with other magnanimous men. However, we shall see below that Jenkins acknowledges that Churchill's White House visit in late 1941 to early 1942 contradicts his own view.

7   Ibid., 651.

8   Jon Meacham, *Franklin and Winston*, 350–51.

having what he also calls the "daemon in man" that bubbles up from within and beyond each statesman's humanity. This enables him, like a Platonic demiurge, to "order and design with a sense almost of infallibility [and] draw out from hazard and confusion."[9] Just as during their times together they frequently "capped each other's stories" in generous conversation,[10] Churchill's speech to Parliament was the closing chapter of their friendship. They enjoyed each other and enjoyed the script of world history they both wrote and were written upon.

Realpolitik and the Friendship of Great-Souled Men

The friendship of Roosevelt and Churchill is paradoxical. On the one hand, they genuinely loved one another. They were virtue-friends, in the Aristotelian sense, as far as two great-souled men can be who devote their lives to action. Indeed, Churchill displayed superiority to Roosevelt by the depth to which he reflected upon the nature of politics in general, and on the totalitarian nature of Stalin's regime in particular. He was able to see the evil in Stalin more clearly than did Roosevelt.[11] He also thought Roosevelt naïve for underestimating Stalin's plans for expansion into Europe. For example, Roosevelt wished to invade the south of France; Churchill feared this would make it impossible for the United States and Great Britain to prevent Stalin from taking Vienna and extending his reach even further into western Europe. On the other hand, as great-souled statesmen, they each led independent nations with separate though overlapping national interests. Their virtue-friendship formed and sustained their mutual work and alliance, and even enabled them to weld their two nations' military staffs into a single operational unit. As statesmen, they engaged in the tough business of running a war and geostrategic planning. They dealt with matters of the highest

9 Churchill, *Marlborough*, I. 569–70. See also his description of the burning flame in Moses ("Moses: the Leader of a People," in *Thoughts and Adventures*, 305).

10 Meacham, *Franklin and Winston*, 165.

11 See Solzhenitsyn's satirical presentation of Eleanor Roosevelt touring the Soviet prisons while wearing her ideological blinkers (*The First Circle*, Chapter 59).

political, moral, and existential importance for nations, which required considerable fortitude. Few are capable of operating at this high summit.

Considerations of realpolitik suggest their friendship was merely a mask, a cover for each man's ruthless and Machiavellian pursuit of his national interests. For example, consider Lend-Lease, regarded by many as a great act of American generosity and friendship for Great Britain. Yet Britain paid dearly for Lend-Lease with the liquidation of British assets in the United States: "[the] British were to be squeezed until they popped and divested of just about everything they had left in America and elsewhere. While he was prepared to extend an immediate credit of $1 billion, Roosevelt insisted that Britain 'must put a couple of billion' up front 'as collateral.'"[12] This was not due to Roosevelt alone, as he had to sway anti-British and isolationist elements in Congress who required Britain pay a steep price for U.S. help. Churchill's response to Lend-Lease was that, "we are not only to be skinned, but flayed to the bone."[13] Such great costs to Britain for American generosity lead some commentators, including Jeremy Havardi, to argue that most of the acts of apparent friendship by the United States were in fact highly self-interested and a means to undermine the British empire.

Furthermore, each man sent spies or "emissaries" to gain crucial information on the other and his situation. Churchill sent Gerald Wilkinson as his personal emissary to General Patton in part to gauge Patton's strength and intentions, because at the time Patton was seen as a possible presidential rival to Roosevelt. For his part, Roosevelt sent William Philips to India to gauge opposition to Britain, but out of deference to Churchill did not provide the support the opposition requested. Each man's use of the dark arts of spying and intelligence also paints a picture of ruthlessness under the cover of civilized friendship. The British broke American codes and secretly read their communications throughout the war. They knew that Hitler had called off his plan to invade England as

12 David J. Bercuson and Holger H. Herwig, *One Christmas in Washington: The Secret Meeting between Roosevelt and Churchill That Changed the World*, 30.

13 Jeremy Havardi, *The Greatest Briton: Essays on Winston Churchill's Life and Political Philosophy*, 216, quoting Martin Gilbert, *Churchill and America*, 208.

early as January 1940. They refrained from sharing this information with the Americans, including Harry Hopkins, Roosevelt's personal emissary, during his first visit to Britain. They did this to keep pressure on the Americans to enter the war.[14]

Do the costs of Lend-Lease and the extensive secrets they kept from one another constitute sufficient evidence that their friendship was largely irrelevant to the considerations of statecraft that brought the two nations together? David Stafford argues that these very goals of statecraft, and the fact they could overcome these obstacles, mark the greatness of these two men and their friendship: "it took a remarkable degree of personal trust in Roosevelt for [Churchill] to clear the ground by confessing so frankly in 1942, in one of their late-night White House chats, that before Pearl Harbor his experts had been breaking American codes."[15] Indeed, their friendship enabled the two countries to share a considerable amount of intelligence, perhaps more than what each held back for itself. Their friendship did not dissolve their differing national interests, but it did enable them at least to manage them and to enjoy a productive working relationship.

Their friendship also served as an example for their respective military staffs, who were initially indifferent or actively contemptuous of the other side, to harmonize their work and, in the case of George Marshall and John Dill, to become close friends themselves.[16] Stafford weighs the great political matters and obstacles of national interest each man faced, and concludes that it was because of such issues that their friendship was both genuine and great: "Such episodes only reinforce the conclusion that the strong personal link between Churchill and Roosevelt was vital to wartime Anglo-American relations."[17] More than their shared heritage of the "English-speaking peoples," "[a] rich hinterland

---

14 David Stafford, *Roosevelt and Churchill: Men of Secrets*, 22.

15 Ibid., xxi.

16 On the leadership role of their friendship, see Bercuson and Herwig, *One Christmas in Washington: The Secret Meeting Between Roosevelt and Churchill That Changed the World*; Alex Danchev, *Very Special Relationship: Field Marshall Sir John Dill and the Anglo-American Alliance, 1941–44*.

17 Stafford, *Roosevelt and Churchill: Men of Secrets*, xxiii.

of personal and political difference thus scarred the landscape between them. It helps neither man, nor history, to pretend otherwise. Fantasies about their personal relations, or about Churchill's American ancestry, or about some innate Anglo-American intimacy, paradoxically only diminish the stature of the two men. For their true achievement lay in overcoming the real and powerful obstacles that stood between them."[18]

It is for reasons such as these that, when describing the great-souled man, Aristotle points out that he concerns himself with only the greatest practical matters, and "is not capable of leading his life to suit anyone else, other than a friend." The magnanimous man, who is autonomous to a very large degree, has few friends because there are so few individuals worthy of his greatness.[19] But when he makes a friend, he holds onto him with absolute loyalty.

Andrew Roberts summarizes the paradoxical friendship of Churchill and Roosevelt in the following words: "Historians too have been fascinated, and perhaps infected, by the idea of this friendship as being the ultimate lynchpin of the Western Alliance. In fact the realities of realpolitik, often in the persons of Marshall and Brooke, constantly intruded on the relationship. When their countries' interests required Roosevelt and Churchill to be friends, they genuinely became so; when they needed to clash, they no less genuinely did that too. Yet unity of action was too great a prize to be jeopardized by lack of charm, especially from two of the most naturally engaging politicians of their era."[20] Conrad Black similarly confirms the importance of their friendship as the cement of the alliance, even as American power grew and the power of the British empire waned: "Yet Roosevelt and Churchill knew each other well, were liberal politicians, saviours of their countries and of their shared civilization. They were united by reciprocal admiration and had scaled history's greatest heights. Their alliance was fading somewhat, but their friendship, like a good and durable marriage, though less exuberant than in years past, was profound and vital."[21]

---

18 Ibid., xviii.
19 Aristotle, *Nicomachean Ethics*, 1125a1.
20 Andrew Roberts, *Masters and Commanders*, 574.
21 Conrad Black, *Franklin Delano Roosevelt: Champion of Freedom*, 1085.

Meacham points to a passage in Churchill's novel, *Savrola*, that illustrates the way each man regarded the possibilities of friendship in statecraft. In it Churchill describes how the possibility of alliance emerges when, over the long course of human history moving toward civilization, man becomes a social animal:

> When the human race was emerging from the darkness of its origin and half-animal, half-human creatures trod the earth, there was no idea of justice, honesty, or virtue, only the motive power which we may call the "will to live." Then perhaps it was a minor peculiarity of some of these early ancestors of man to combine in twos and threes for their mutual protection. The first alliance was made; the combinations prospered where the isolated individuals failed. [22]

By "will to live," Churchill appears to refer to a Machiavellian acquisitiveness for power and domination (as well as survival), which alone is an insufficient and even unstable basis for the "minor peculiarity" of cooperation required for the creation and maintenance of international alliances. Moral virtue is needed to produce a more durable bond.

After a certain point, alliances depend not simply on mutual advantage that offers protection, but on "the members keeping faith with each other, on the practice of honesty, justice, and the rest of the virtues. Only those beings in whom such faculties were present were able to combine, and thus only the relatively honest men were preserved." Meacham cites a comparable statement by Roosevelt to show he was of a similar mind: "Friendship among nations, as among individuals, calls for constructive efforts to muster the forces of humanity

22 Meacham, *Franklin and Winston*, 119, citing *Savrola: A Tale of the Revolution in Laurania*, 84–85. For Churchill's developed view of the meaning of civilization, see "Civilisation." See also Daniel J. Mahoney, *The Conservative Foundations of the Liberal Order*, 74–84, and Sandys and Henley, *God and Churchill*, 118–30. I thank Professor Mahoney for pointing out the importance of this speech to me.

in order that an atmosphere of close understanding and cooperation may be cultivated."[23]

If we make allowances for the intellectually dubious Whiggism behind Churchill's historicism in *Savrola*, we can see that for both creative statesmen, political alliance—"close understanding and cooperation"—depends upon the virtues, the "forces of humanity." Alliances presuppose the good character and friendship of leaders. Indeed, Churchill's statement especially compares with Aristotle's description of virtue-friendship as consisting of the full presence of the virtues. It follows too that failing to act virtuously corrodes and perhaps severely threatens alliances and the trust upon which they depend. This might be especially true for Churchill, for whom moral virtue, as well as the related skills of conversation and being agreeable dining partners, were paramount.

In pursuing national interests, including spying and imposing high costs for Lend-Lease, the two men played a high-risk game in the name of national interest and necessity, and perhaps even for the common good of their alliance. Such are the "obstacles" and "great deeds" over which great-souled friends interact. That they played this high-risk game at the highest levels reinforces Stafford's assessment of their friendship and places it within the proper theoretical framework. To be great friends they had not only to be great allies, but also to be great rivals for power. How else could they respect and love each other?

Friendship Disrupted by Tyrannical Eros at Teheran

The dynamics of the two men's friendship and their respective pursuits of national interest can be seen throughout their relationship, but nowhere more clearly than in the drama of the "Big Three" meeting at Teheran, November 28 to December 1, 1943. Churchill and Roosevelt composed two-thirds of the "Big Three" during World War Two who allied to defeat Hitler and Nazism. Churchill and Roosevelt were close allies because they were leaders of the English-speaking peoples; but

---

23 Meacham, *Franklin and Winston*, 119–20, citing *Public Papers and Addresses of Franklin D. Roosevelt*, vol. II, 130.

more than that, they were also good friends whose friendship facilitated their alliance. One might also say their alliance at certain instances served their friendship. A brief overview of their relations between 1940 and 1945 easily confirms this. They spent numerous hours together during the war and they were evidently fond of one another. However, they were both statesmen who led their sovereign nations with interests particular to each, regardless of their overlap. For all the shared principles of the English-speaking peoples, Roosevelt disdained the British Empire that Churchill sought to defend, and he also recognized that the United States and the Soviet Union would dominate the post-war world. After the Big Three conference in Teheran in 1943, Churchill lamented, "I realized at Teheran for the first time what a small nation we are . . . . There I sat with the great Russian bear on one side of me, with paws outstretched, and on the other side sat the great American buffalo, and between the two sat the poor little English donkey who was the only one, the only one of the three, who knew the right way home."[24]

Churchill's goal of protecting the British Empire would have to give way to playing a smaller role in the post-war world. Thus national interest and *raison d'etat* was a strong undercurrent in their friendship. Moreover, as statesmen, each was an actor on the stage of world politics who portrayed himself as he wished to be seen.[25] Roosevelt is well known for maintaining emotional distance from everyone, even those closest to him, including his wife Eleanor. This distance earned him the nickname, "American sphinx." Churchill is generally regarded as more transparent and "limpid" (his daughter's phrase), but even there one must be cautious not to over-estimate this side of him. As Jonathan Rose demonstrates, Churchill very much regarded himself an actor on the world stage who "deconstructed and collapsed the distinction between theatre and reality, between melodramatic gesture and sincerity . . . . [T]hat 'acting naturally' is either impossible or a bore: the human personality must be

---

24 Meacham, *Franklin and Winston*, 259, citing Colville to John Wheeler-Bennett, *Action This Day: Working with Churchill*, 96.
25 For a general treatment of such diplomatic acting, see Schabert, *How World Politics is Made*.

consciously constructed as a work of dramatic art."[26] Or as Meacham writes: "On afternoons like this one in Washington (1942), or on the deck of the Prince of Wales the previous August, these two political actors were, in a way, designing the stage set of modern politics."[27]

It is with these considerations in mind that we consider an important episode in the friendship of Roosevelt and Churchill that illuminates the tension between their virtue-friendship and the realpolitik national interests that they, as leaders of their respective great powers, had to assert and protect.

We focus on the meeting of the Big Three at Teheran that ran from November 28 to December 1, 1943. This was the first of two such meetings (they met at Yalta in February 1944, and Roosevelt died before the final meeting in Potsdam in July/August 1945). Churchill and Roosevelt by this time had cemented their friendship which they had initiated in Argentia in 1940, continued during Churchill's lengthy stays in Washington (December 1941–January 1942), Casablanca in January 1943, and over the course of their massive correspondence with one another. Their personal friendship had blossomed over that time, as did their political alliance whose most "friendly" gestures included Land-Lease (though this still cost Great Britain immensely) and the donation of 300 Sherman tanks and 100 self-propelled guns after the British lost the Battle of Tobruk in June 1942. Meacham explains the turn of events and quite possibly their friendship at Teheran: "In Teheran, the bill for Churchill's seduction of Roosevelt came due. From the destroyer deal to Lend-Lease, from the shipment of Shermans after Tobruk to cooperation on the atomic bomb, Roosevelt's intimate style of governing had long worked to Churchill's benefit. Now, at a meeting of the Big Three in Teheran, Roosevelt would turn on his old friend."[28]

Teheran was Roosevelt's first meeting with Stalin. Like Churchill, Roosevelt placed supreme importance on what we now call "face time" with world leaders. The workshop of world politics necessitates that

26 Rose, *The Literary Churchill*, 17. Part of Rose's general account of Churchill the actor rests on his 1897 essay, "The Scaffolding of Rhetoric."

27 Meacham, *Franklin and Winston*, 144.

28 Meacham, *Franklin and Winston*, 245.

statesmen face each other as persons. It is a way of getting to know them and to develop camaraderie and indeed friendship so that they can work more easily upon the great political, strategic, and indeed existential problems they face.[29] Roosevelt understood that he and Stalin were to be the primary powers after the war, and it was also of paramount importance for him that Stalin see him as capable of thinking and acting independently of Churchill and of British interests, for Stalin knew of the friendship and alliance between the two men and thus distrusted them.

Roosevelt and Stalin each came to Teheran wishing to charm the other. For all his tyrannical eros, Stalin was capable of being very charming. Indeed, as Simon Sebag Montefiore argues, this was the key to ruling his party: "The foundation of Stalin's power in the Party was not fear: it was charm. Stalin possessed the dominant will among his magnates, but they also found his policies generally congenial . . . . [T]he new archives confirm that his real genius was something different—and surprising: 'he could charm people.' He was what is now known as a 'people person.' While incapable of true empathy on one hand, he was a master of friendships on the other."[30] It is hard to square Montefiore's claim that Stalin was the "master of friendships" with the fact that he dominated them. Susan Butler notes how "he ran the lives of his associates down to the smallest detail," including choosing where they lived and what they drove.[31] Of course he also chose when many of them were to be executed. Stalin's mastery of friendships and of friends fits with his famous paranoia. His view of friendship is perhaps expressed best by his favorite aphorism by his beloved Georgian national poet, Shota Rustaveli: "A close friend turned out to be an enemy more dangerous than a foe."[32]

Of course, it is unbelievable that Stalin became such a powerful tyrant on the basis of fear alone. Charm and the capacity to be loved is certainly an important basis for rule. Indeed he was charming toward Roosevelt,

---

29   Heyking, "Friendship as Precondition and Consequence of Creativity in Politics"; Schabert, *How World Politics is Made*.
30   Simon Sebag Montefiore, *Stalin: The Court of the Red Tsar*, 49.
31   Susan Butler, *Roosevelt and Stalin: Portrait of a Partnership*, 72.
32   Stephen Kotkin, *Stalin: Paradoxes of Power, 1878–1928*, I. 10.

inspired in large part by the fact that Roosevelt was more powerful than he. Stalin had never met a ruler more powerful than he and, as someone for whom human relations are nothing but power, this would constitute an important incentive to charm. Indeed, this helps explain his disdain toward Churchill, who frequently opposed him.[33] Roosevelt seemed to understand Stalin's concern for power and its appearance. He cultivated it at this meeting, knowing that having grown so powerful, the Soviet Union must be treated "at least as an equal." He manipulated Stalin's craving for respect, for he thought he "suffered from an inferiority complex."[34]

The charm shown by each, of course, was strictly for show and served the purpose of furthering political cooperation between Roosevelt and Stalin, who both sought a spring 1944 date for Operation Overlord. Churchill alone pushed for extended operations in the Mediterranean, which Stalin rightly saw as delaying the opening of the second front, as well as a strategy for the Allies to oppose him in the Balkans, Austria, and Czechoslovakia. Churchill was dismayed that he could not meet with Roosevelt alone in Teheran before the conference because Roosevelt had accepted Stalin's invitation to be housed in the Russian embassy. However, Churchill and Roosevelt were able to meet in Cairo before traveling to Teheran.

Despite Churchill's worries about being left out of Great Power discussions regarding Overlord and post-war plans (which he was, to a large extent), he need never have worried about being fully replaced by Stalin in Roosevelt's orbit. The meetings between Roosevelt and Stalin, while friendly, constituted a dance of masks: the former was a "consummate actor" and the latter "was famous for his sphinxlike inscrutability."[35] For instance, Roosevelt knew staying at the Russian Embassy meant living in bugged rooms. Beria briefed Stalin each morning on what Roosevelt said and did in his rooms. Butler places great weight on Stalin's obsession with bugging Roosevelt's rooms as a way of understanding him, and on Roosevelt's performance while knowing he was always being

---

33 For details on the meeting, see Susan Butler, *Roosevelt and Stalin: Portrait of a Partnership*, 68–148.

34 Frank Costigliola, *Roosevelt's Lost Alliances: How Personal Politics Helped Start the Cold War*, 195.

35 Butler, *Roosevelt and Stalin*, 73.

listened to: "Nothing underlines Stalin's obsessive and thorough nature quite clearly as his daily analysis of Roosevelt's supposedly private words and attitudes. Nothing underlines Roosevelt's ability to size people up correctly, and his talents as an actor, more than his pursuit of the invitation to stay in the Russian embassy and his conduct while there. Stalin learned only what Roosevelt wanted him to learn. Roosevelt would have been tickled pink to know that Stalin didn't dream Roosevelt knew his conversations were being picked up by hidden microphones."[36]

This dance of masks was the means by which Roosevelt and Stalin joined their minds together for common political purposes. But the dance of masks is as much a means as a hindrance of means, which explains Roosevelt's frustrations with the Teheran meeting which he had worked so hard to bring about. These frustrations help explain his subsequent mistreatment of his friend, Churchill. He explained his predicament to his Secretary of Labor (1933–45), Frances Perkins:

> For the first three days I made absolutely no progress. I couldn't get any personal connection with Stalin, although I had done everything he asked me to do. I had stayed at his Embassy, gone to his dinners, been introduced to his ministers and generals. He was correct, stiff, solemn, not smiling, nothing human to get hold of. I felt pretty discouraged. If it was all going to be official paper work, there was no sense in my having made this long journey which the Russians had wanted. They couldn't come to America or any place in Europe for it. I had come there to accommodate Stalin. I felt pretty discouraged because I thought I was making no personal headway. What we were doing could have been done by the foreign ministers.[37]

36 Ibid., 46–47.
37 Frances Perkins, *The Roosevelt I Knew*, 83–84. Roberts points out the connection between Roosevelt's frustration and his subsequent mistreatment, with Stalin, of Churchill (*Masters and Commanders*, 445). See also Meacham, *Franklin and Winston*, 264. Churchill describes his difficulties with making personal contact with Stalin during their first meeting in August 1942 (*The Second World War*, vol. 4, 436–51).

Roosevelt's account differs somewhat from that of Churchill, who mentions at several points that the three of them spoke freely and with friendship throughout the conference, both in the formal proceedings and during the luncheons and dinners.[38]

Even so, Roosevelt's statement to Perkins contains several important points. First, the whole point of these conferences was making a "personal connection." Discussing strategy and tactics and performing related negotiations was the work of "foreign ministers."[39] Or perhaps such lesser work could be achieved by telegram. Face time was of paramount importance for Churchill as well: "We talk over the whole position in every aspect—the military, economic, diplomatic, financial. All—all is examined."[40] "What an ineffectual method of conveying human thought correspondence is . . . telegraphed with all its rapidity, all the facilities of our—modern intercommunication. They are simply dead, blank walls compared to personal—personal contacts."[41] Telegrams, letters, memos, and today emails, can address isolated problems, but only personal meetings enable statesmen to address the "whole world situation," as he explained to Stalin in his letter of January 5, 1945.[42] Only when statesmen meet person-to-person, preferably as friends, can they gain the daimonic perspective of the whole over its parts.[43]

Second, Roosevelt was desperate to accomplish something with Stalin because, despite his physical handicap which caused him immense discomfort and pain, he had travelled a long way first by boat and then by plane (which was quite uncomfortable even for able-bodied individuals at the time) and so had made an enormous personal sacrifice to come to Stalin. Stalin was reputedly afraid of flying, but probably more

38 Churchill, *The Second World War*, vol. 4, 302–60.
39 Former French President François Mitterrand makes a similar observation (Heyking, "Friendship as Precondition and Consequence of Creativity in Politics" 91).
40 Meacham, *Franklin and Winston*, 301, quoting Churchill in Roosevelt, *Complete Presidential Press Conferences of Franklin Delano Roosevelt, 1933–1945*, vol. XXIV, September 16, 1944, 111–16.
41 Ibid., 301–02
42 Quoted in Churchill, *The Second World War*, vol. 6, 294.
43 See below in Chapter Eight.

importantly, he was also a tyrant whose movements were restricted by having an enormous security detail that catered both to real and perceived threats.

This leads to the third point about Roosevelt's statement to Perkins. Roosevelt had the formidable task in this short period of time of having to forge a "personal connection" with Stalin. If Churchill was an actor and Roosevelt was the "American sphinx," the impenetrability of Stalin's personality was exponentially greater and murkier. As a tyrant, he was, as Plato has Socrates claim of tyrannical eros, "someone who's insane and unbalanced [and who] tries to rule not only human beings but gods as well, and thinks he can."[44] Alexander Solzhenitsyn's portrayal of him as Dante's Satan, whose heart is ice-cold, captures this impenetrability and paranoia: "Mistrust was Iosif Djugashvili's determining trait. Mistrust was his world view."[45] Roosevelt faced significant obstacles in attempting to make a "connection" with him. Thus Harry Hopkins' excitement when Roosevelt decided that Stalin was indeed "get-atable."[46]

---

44 Plato, *Republic*, 573c. Plato's "ancient" tyrant differs from "modern" scientific tyrants like Stalin, but they share this ambition to rule human beings and gods as well. See Manfred Henningsen, "The Dream Worlds of Tyrants," 131–46.

45 Alexander Solzhenitsyn, *The First Circle*, 105. Solzhenitsyn goes on to suggest that the only one Stalin ever trusted was Hitler when he signed the Molotov-Ribbentrop treaty, and for which the Soviet Union paid dearly when Germany later invaded. Churchill criticizes Stalin for his naiveté toward Hitler: "War is mainly a catalogue of blunders, but it may be doubted whether any mistake in history has equaled that of which Stalin and the Communist chiefs were guilty when they cast away all possibilities in the Balkans and supinely awaited, or were incapable of realizing, the fearful onslaught which impended upon Russia. We have hitherto rated them as selfish calculators. In this period they were proved simpletons as well . . . . Stalin and his commissars showed themselves at this moment the most completely outwitted bunglers of the Second World War" (Churchill, *The Second World War*, vol. 3, 316). Churchill complains throughout *The Second World War* of Stalin's mendacity (e.g., ibid., 49) and his self-delusions and lack of contact with reality (ibid., 328, 411).

46 Frank Costigliola, *Roosevelt's Lost Alliances*, 198–99.

We return to Roosevelt's report to Perkins: "I thought it over all night and made up my mind I had to do something desperate . . . . I couldn't stay in Teheran forever. I had to cut through this icy surface so that later I could talk by telephone or letter in a personal way. I had scarcely seen Churchill alone during the conference. I had a feeling that the Russians did not feel right about seeing us conferring together in a language which we understood and they didn't."[47] The Russians, especially Stalin, were distrustful and it was imperative for Roosevelt, on the third day of his first meeting with Stalin, to "cut through this icy surface" by doing "something desperate."

"On my way to the conference room that morning we caught up with Winston and I had just a moment to say to him, 'Winston, I hope you won't be sore at me for what I am going to do.' Winston just shifted his cigar and grunted. I must say he behaved very decently afterward."[48] At least Roosevelt apologized to Churchill in advance for risking their friendship for the sake of the Big Three alliance, which would in fact entail shoving Great Britain, and Churchill, to the curb.

Roosevelt explains to Perkins:

> I began almost as soon as we got into the conference room. I talked privately with Stalin . . . . Then I said, lifting my hand up to cover a whisper (which of course had to be interpreted), "Winston is cranky this morning, he got up on the wrong side of his bed." A vague smile passed over Stalin's eyes, and I decided I was on the right track. As soon as I sat down at the conference table, I began to tease Churchill about his Britishness, about John Bull, about his cigars, about his habits. It began to register with Stalin. Winston got red and scowled, and the more he did so, the more Stalin smiled. Finally Stalin broke out into a deep, hearty guffaw, and for the first time in three days *I saw light.* I kept it up until Stalin was laughing with me, and it was then that I called him "Uncle Joe." He would have thought me fresh the day before, but that day he

---

47 Perkins, *The Roosevelt I Knew*, 84; Meacham, *Franklin and Winston*, 264.
48 Perkins, *The Roosevelt I Knew*, 84.

laughed and came over and shook my hand. From that time on our relations were personal, and Stalin himself indulged in occasional witticism. The ice was broken and we talked like men and brothers.[49]

Roosevelt had gambled to connect to the tyrannical soul in Stalin and it paid off.

Roosevelt and Stalin had teased Churchill the previous evening by appearing to endorse a policy of liquidating the German officer corps as post-war punishment. This infuriated Churchill so much that he had to leave the reception room to cool off. Churchill writes in *The Second World War* that when Stalin and Molotov approached him with broad grins, with Stalin exercising his "captivating manner" to a greater extent than Churchill had ever seen before, he was unconvinced "all was chaff and there was no serious intent lurking behind."[50] Combined with his general sense of being "left out" at this conference, he would have been in ill-humour to receive this kind of treatment from his friend at the start of the next day. No wonder his daughter, Mary Soames, judged, "My father was awfully wounded at Teheran. For reasons of state, it seems to me President Roosevelt was out to charm Stalin, and my father was the odd man out. He felt that very keenly . . . . My father was very hurt, I think."[51]

This episode of high diplomacy is low comedy. Roosevelt resorted to school boy antics of teasing his good friend Churchill to cut through the icy surface of the tyrant, in order to achieve aims of the national interest and of the alliance. He had to tease Churchill as schoolboys tease

---

49   Ibid., 84 (emphasis added); Meacham, 265. Churchill mentions none of this in his *The Second World War*, except to say that the "private contact" between Roosevelt and Stalin throughout the conference led him to seek his own one-on-one time with Stalin (*The Second World War,* vol. 4, 331).

50   Churchill, *The Second World War*, vol. 4, 330.

51   Meacham, *Franklin and Winston*, 265–66, quoting from interview with Mary Soames. Unsurprisingly, Churchill reports that at the conclusion of the conference, "we separated in an atmosphere of friendship and unity of purpose, I personally was well content" (*The Second World War*, vol. 5, 358).

and can mercilessly "leave out" boys as a means of managing in-group dynamics. This is the law of the schoolyard and it is the law of the tribe. But it is not the law of civilized peoples that Churchill, long ago in his *Savrola* novel, described as "keeping faith with each other, on the practice of honesty, justice, and the rest of the virtues." In terms of these laws of civility, and in light of Churchill's understanding of the demands of friendship, Roosevelt took an enormous risk by reverting to the law of the "half-animal, half human creatures." It took Churchill to behave "very decently afterward" to leaven Roosevelt's sojourn in this less-than civilized territory, as necessary as it was.

But Roosevelt judged the risk of rupturing these bonds worthwhile because of the magnitude of the task. He had to cut through Stalin's icy soul and make a connection so that he could more easily work with him. Even though he risked Churchill's friendship in doing so, it is more likely that his friendship with Churchill actually enabled him to tease him. Their friendship gave him the freedom to pursue national interests as well as the good of the alliance, even if it meant risking it by pushing its limits. Indeed, for spirited and great-souled statesmen as these two men, such teasing and roughhousing actually forms part of the dynamics of their friendships. Perkins explains: "He teased Churchill unmercifully, but that was a sign of his being 'in the family.' It was Roosevelt's habit to indulge in friendly teasing bouts, and he expected to get back as good as he gave."[52] While the alliance would likely still have remained intact had the two men not been friends and Roosevelt had teased Churchill, it is very likely that their alliance would have suffered because of the diminished trust and collegiality between them. Roosevelt had to walk on a fine tightrope, but their friendship made it easier for him to cross to safety. As Meacham notes, "Aside from the politics of the alliance, there was a personal bond at work that, though often tested, held them together."[53] Roosevelt's risk bore fruit. When they met a few months later in Yalta, "the two leaders greeted each other as old friends," with Stalin smiling, which he rarely did.[54]

---

52 Perkins, *The Roosevelt I Knew*, 80–81.
53 Meacham, *Franklin and Winston*, 270.
54 Ibid., 316.

Statesmanship is rough business. This is one of its main attractions for great-souled men, including Churchill and Roosevelt. The risks are great but so are the rewards, and among these great rewards are great friendships that such men actively seek. We turn now to consider how their friendship was forged.

Chapter Five
Churchill and Roosevelt Overseeing
the Whole Scene

I must be with you when you see the sunset on the snows of
the Atlas Mountains.[1]

Harry Hopkins: Friendly Intermediary

Churchill and Roosevelt had their first meeting as world leaders at Argentia, off the coast of Newfoundland, in August 1940. Their correspondence by that time was well-established and through it they had
established a high degree of friendliness, though even by January 1942
Churchill would still regard them as the "early days of our friendship"
when he then nervously asked Harry Hopkins how Roosevelt had responded to a possible faux-pas by Churchill.[2]

Hopkins was the key intermediary between the two men and
Churchill's assessment of him is indicative of the standards by which he
judged individuals and the importance of friendship for statecraft. He
met Hopkins when Roosevelt sent him in January 1940 to gain a sense
of Churchill's character:

> Thus I met Harry Hopkins, that extraordinary man, who
> played, and was to play, a sometimes decisive part in the
> whole movement of the war. His was a soul that flamed out
> of a frail and failing body. He was a crumbling lighthouse

1   Churchill to Roosevelt, cited in Churchill, *The Second World War*, vol. 4,
    621.
2   Churchill, *The Second World War*, vol. 3, 617.

from which there shone the beams that led great fleets to harbor. He had also a gift of sardonic humour. I always enjoyed his company, especially when things went ill. He could also be very disagreeable and say hard and sour things. My experiences were teaching me to be able to do this too, if need be. At our first meeting we were about three hours together and I soon comprehended his personal dynamism and the outstanding importance of his mission . . . . With gleaming eye and quiet . . . . And from this hour began a friendship between us which sailed serenely over all earthquakes and convulsions . . . . In the history of the United States few brighter flames have burned.[3]

By mentioning Hopkins' "gleaming eye," his flaming soul, "personal dynamism," and his bright-burning flame, Churchill appeals to the classical language of *gloria*, the language of daimonism and heroism, to assess Hopkins' character and his capacity to serve as intermediary between Roosevelt and himself. It is this daimonism he saw in Roosevelt as well and was the main characteristic that made statesmen great as well as capable of forging close ties of friendship. These are the same categories he used to describe Moses, as discussed in Chapter Two.

Indeed it was Hopkins who was sent by Roosevelt to size up Churchill and judge his character. It was only part of his task to determine whether Churchill had the seriousness and fortitude to deserve American military support. He also had to determine whether Churchill, the supporter of the British Empire, shared a similar philosophy about freedom and good government that could sustain world order after the defeat of Nazism.[4] He ended up staying six weeks in England, during which time he endeared himself to Churchill and his circle.[5] Near the end of his visit, Hopkins told Churchill what he was going to report back to Roosevelt: "Well, I'm going to quote you one verse from that Book

---

3   Ibid., 20–21.
4   Meacham, *Franklin and Winston*, 89.
5   Costigliola captures Hopkins' charm and the emotional responses of Churchill and others (*Roosevelt's Lost Alliances*, 99–108).

of Books . . . : 'Whither thou goest, I will go; and where thou lodgest, I will lodge: thy people shall be my people, and thy God my God.' Then, quietly, 'Even to the end.'"[6] Churchill wept in response. Pamela Harriman reports that it was because of Hopkins that, when Roosevelt and Churchill met, they were "able to meet as old friends."[7]

Argentia: Forging the Friendship in Festivity

The meeting of Roosevelt and Churchill at Argentia, off the coast of Newfoundland, was the first step in bringing the two great nations together. Peter H. Russell judges that "The meeting forged that bond of heart and soul and trust without which the grand alliance could not have accomplished its ends."[8] It not only gave the two men an opportunity to meet one another. It also introduced senior members of each other's military staffs to one another. It was a carefully choreographed event mostly on the part of Churchill, who planned its central ceremony, the church service on the deck of the H.M.S. *Prince of Wales*. While Roosevelt wished to use the meeting to pronounce a vision of the post-war world, the meeting in fact had no agenda. It was to be a time of some informality, to forge friendships: "The main business of this first lunch was to organize the business of the conference. Their basic approach was to have a conference that was open and fluid with a minimum of organization. The military and diplomatic personae would pair off and talk shop about matters of mutual concern. There would be no overall agenda or coordination of talks. The Prime Minister and President would do most of their talking over lunches and dinners."[9] A sign of its importance for Roosevelt is the fact that his first visit to the deck of the H.M.S. *Prince of Wales* likely constituted the longest walk he had taken since he was stricken with polio.[10]

Roosevelt told his son, "If nothing else had happened while we were there, that would have cemented us."[11] As the first personal meeting as

6   Meacham, *Franklin and Winston*, 94. Hopkins cited Ruth 1:16.
7   Ibid., 98.
8   Peter H. Russell, *The First Summit and the Atlantic Charter*, 42.
9   Ibid., 19.
10   Ibid., 20.
11   Ibid., 22.

war leaders between the two men who had already had extensive correspondence, the meeting achieved Churchill's central goal. David Bercuson and Holger Holwig report: "The most important result of the conference as far as Churchill was concerned was an intangible one, as he later reported to the War Cabinet. 'The Prime Minister said that he had got on intimate terms with the President. Of the six meals they had had together, five had been on the President's ship.'"[12] Above whatever material support the Americans could offer him, Churchill sought Roosevelt's friendship and believed he had received it.

One of the most significant events of the Argentia meeting was the worship service on the deck of the H.M.S. *Prince of Wales*. Churchill planned it, including the hymns, on the trip across the Atlantic.[13] He attended to numerous details immediately before the service, including moving chairs to their proper places on the desk and pulling out the folds of the Union Jack.[14] Indeed, Churchill frequently immersed himself in the details when it came to these sorts of events. Cita Stelzer explains how, when he had friends and political associates over for dinner, he paid strict attention to seating arrangements, frequently having political rivals sit next to one another. This was a detail he learned from his mother.[15]

Roosevelt referred to the worship service as the "keynote" of the meeting. During the service the British and Americans were "completely intermingled." They worshipped the same God, they listened to the same sermon, and they sang the same hymns as a way of marrying the two services, the two nations, together: "British and American Marine personnel intermingled in one mass on the huge quarter deck. It was noticeable that we all seemed to know the words of the hymns . . . ."[16] Morton writes that during the war "there had been no scene like this, a scene, it seemed, from another world, conceived on lines different from

12 Bercuson and Herwig, *One Christmas in Washington,* 34, citing Churchill, *The Churchill War Papers*, vol. 3, 1081.

13 H. V. Morton, *Atlantic Meeting*, 100–01.

14 Ibid., 110. He also helped to organize and coach the rehearsals for receiving Roosevelt onto the *Prince of Wales* for their initial meeting (ibid., 84).

15 Cita Stelzer, *Dinner With Churchill*, 30.

16 Bercuson and Herwig, *One Christmas in Washington,* 28, citing General Sir Leslie Hollis, *One Marine's Tale*, 82

anything known to the pageant-masters of the Axis, a scene rooted in the first principles of European civilization which go back to the figure of Charlemagne kneeling before the Pope on Christmas morning."[17]

The hymns included "O God our help in Ages Past," "Onward Christian Soldiers," and "Eternal Father Strong to Save." "O God Our Help in Ages Past" was written by Isaac Watts and paraphrases Psalm 90 by calling upon God for "shelter from the stormy blast." It was also sung at Churchill's funeral as his coffin was withdrawn from St. Paul's Cathedral.[18] Later in a radio broadcast, he explained why he chose "Onward Christian Soldiers" by Sabine Baring-Gould:

> We sang "Onward, Christian Soldiers" indeed, and I felt that this was no vain presumption, but that we had the right to feel that we serving a cause for the sake of which a trumpet has sounded from on high. When I looked upon that densely packed congregation of fighting men of the same language, of the same faith, of the same fundamental laws, of the same ideals . . . it swept across me that here was the only hope, but also the sure hope, of saving the world from measureless degradation.[19]

Finally, "Eternal Father Strong to Save" by William Whiting is a hymn popular with navies because of its themes of dangers at sea.

John Martin, Churchill's secretary, stated that "It seemed a sort of marriage service between the two navies."[20] Meacham explains that the worship service was an instance of using "the dramatic to convince people of a reality they cannot see."[21] The service is an instance of the cultic or festive aspect of statesmanship and political friendship whose mean-

---

17 Morton, *Atlantic Meeting*, 113–14.

18 Andrew Roberts, "The death of Winston Churchill was the day the Empire died," *The Telegraph*, January 18, 2015 (http://www.telegraph.co.uk/history/11351639/The-death-of-Winston-Churchill-was-the-day-the-Empire-died.html).

19 Ace Collins, *Stories Behind the Hymns That Inspire America*, 153–54.

20 Quoted in Martin Gilbert, *Churchill and America*, 231.

21 Meacham, *Franklin and Winston*, 115.

ing Plato first expounded when he recognized the manner in which choral performance is the essence of political friendship.[22] For Plato as much as for Churchill, politics is not simply about performing great deeds. It is about story-telling, myths, and ritual. These tell the stories of great deeds, but, indeed, those stories themselves are great actions for they bring clarity and order to the chaos and shifting images and perceptions that constitute normal political life. It is a major reason Churchill wrote so much. His great ancestor, the Duke of Marlborough, was content with the monument of Blenheim Palace, but Churchill knew that words were more immortal.[23] Choruses, as Plato describes them in the *Laws*, constitute the highest manner that citizens participate in the great deeds and virtues of their polity. In festivity, they reenact, in body and soul, the virtues of their polity. They do so in chorus, like the British and American sailors on the *Prince of Wales*, because chorus is a consummate expression of political friendship. Churchill's own sense of pomp and circumstance is a reflection of this ancient Platonic-Aristotelian insight regarding the liturgical essence of political friendship.

Washington: Living Together and Sharing Conversation and Thinking

Churchill's extended visit to Washington in December 1941 to January 1942, where he stayed at the White House, helped forge their friendship because it enabled the two men to spend their days, as Aristotle says, "living together and sharing conversation and thinking."[24] Jenkins, who contends the two men were not really friends, regards Churchill's visit "one of the most bizarre interludes in the history of relations between heads of state and government. It remains a standing contradiction of my view, expressed in the previous chapter, that great stars are only happy in their own unimpeded orbits. The White House . . . is indeed a mansion, but to insert into it a second head of

22 Plato, *Laws*, Book II. For discussion and analysis, see my *The Form of Politics*, chapter 6.
23 See Chapter Nine below.
24 Aristotle, *Nicomachean Ethics*, 1170b10–12.

government with entourage was to make conditions almost hugger-mugger. At first Churchill had intended to stay only about a week, but as his visit lengthened he became near to a real-life version of *The Man Who Came to Dinner*. There was no indication that his welcome wore thin."[25]

This was the period in which, in Anne Curzon-Howe's recollection, they "seemed to be getting on famously and capping each other's stories."[26] Mary Soames described them together as "like sitting between two lions roaring at the same time."[27] While Churchill describes these as still the "early days of our friendship,"[28] they gained profound knowledge of each other's goals and of one another. Churchill's description describes the mixture of work and play during their time together:

> We saw each other for several hours every day, and lunched always together, with Harry Hopkins as a third. We talked of nothing but business, and reached a great measure of agreement on many points, both large and small. Dinner was a more social occasion, but equally intimate and friendly. The President punctiliously made the preliminary cocktails himself, and I wheeled him in his chair from the drawing-room to the lift as a mark of respect. . . . I formed a very strong affection, which grew with our years of comradeship, for this formidable politician who had imposed his will for nearly ten years upon the American scene, and whose heart seemed to respond to many of the impulses that stirred my own. As we both, by need or habit, were forced to do much of our work in bed, he visited me in my room whenever he felt inclined, and encouraged me to do the same to him.[29]

25 Jenkins, *Churchill: A Biography*, 671–72.
26 Quoted in Meacham, *Franklin and Winston*, 165.
27 Ibid., 5.
28 Churchill, *The Second World War*, vol. 4, 617.
29 Ibid., 587–88.

The familiarity and intimacy the two men shared gave rise to perhaps the most famous anecdote of Churchill's time at the White House. The two men were working on the United Nations Declaration. They were desperate to complete it and to have Stalin sign it in order to coordinate their planning for the Far East theater of war, as this was immediately after the attack on Pearl Harbor. Drawing from Hopkins' account of the episode, Doris Kearns Goodwin reports that Roosevelt had completed the text and excitedly burst into Churchill's quarters, where he found him naked and getting out of the bathtub. Undoubtedly embarrassed, Roosevelt apologized for the intrusion, but Churchill's reported response is priceless: "The president apologized and said he would come back at a better time. No need to go, Churchill said: 'The Prime Minister of Great Britain has nothing to conceal from the President of the United States.'"[30] Costigliola reports on other similar incidents during Churchill's visit, and their likely significance: "Odd as it may have been, such nudity likely fostered a sense of intimacy and trust as they discussed intelligence secrets and atomic research."[31] Like Plato's guardians whose bodies and souls are naked to one another as an expression of political friendship, Churchill understood the moral obligations of friendship. Churchill later denied this event had occurred to Robert Sherwood, Hopkins' biographer, pointing out that he never received Roosevelt in anything less than a towel.[32] Churchill seems to have been joking with Sherwood, which suggests the episode did in fact occur. Indeed, Churchill states at the beginning of his description of his time in Washington that "the whirls of events and the personal tasks I had to perform that my memory till refreshed had preserved but a vague impression of these days."[33] Hopkins' memory is thus perhaps more reliable.

30 Doris Kearns Goodwin, *No Ordinary Time: Franklin and Eleanor Roosevelt: The Home Front in World War II*, 312.

31 Costigliola, *Roosevelt's Lost Alliances*, 155. Paul Johnson notes how George W. Bush and Tony Blair initiated their friendship in the gymnasium of the Kananaskis Lodge in Alberta during the G8 meeting of 2002 (Paul Johnson, "Indispensable Friendship").

32 Bercuson and Herwig, *One Christmas in Washington*, 220.

33 Churchill, *The Second World War*, vol. 4, 587.

Moreover, Churchill was not entirely modest, as he frequently went naked when swimming and when he was in his quarters.[34] He seems to have regarded such indifference to bodily appearance a sign of greatness in a leader, as he notes Marlborough frequently bathed and went to the bathroom in the open.[35] Waller Newell summarizes this vision of leadership in Churchill: "boyish ingenuousness and inability to conceal his ambition. Although Churchill could play the role of populist, his aristocratic background bred in him a contempt for artifice or concealment that is consistent with the code of the gentleman stretching back to Aristotle and Cicero. This code—which holds that a gentleman never stoops to dishonesty because he stands in need of no one's good opinion so badly that he would lie to achieve it—was part and parcel of Churchill's demeanor."[36] Churchillian magnanimity includes indifference or contempt for "artifice" which extended at times to appearance (though his choice of clothing and his famous cigars were part of a carefully crafted image).

Churchill and Roosevelt's days together also served as an example for their top military commanders. Members of each leader's General Staff had strong contempt for the other side. The Americans thought the British stuffy and imperialistic; the British thought the Americans inexperienced and brash. Each side brought its own image of the other nation with them.[37] Their friendship served as an example to ease the rivalries and tensions between the two General Staffs, to the point where many fine friendships were created: "I am sure their close relationships were necessary for the conduct of the war, and I could not have grasped the whole position without them."[38] The friendship of Marshall and Dill is perhaps the most important and Churchill notes how important these friendships were to facilitating the joint operations of the two countries.

Churchill's visit to Washington brought about two key contributions to its war effort from the Americans. The first was his success in

34   Ibid., 402; Meacham, *Franklin and Winston*, 51.
35   Churchill, *Marlborough*, vol. 2, 300.
36   Waller Newell, *The Soul of a Leader*, 49.
37   Bercuson and Holwig, *One Christmas in Washington*.
38   Churchill, *The Second World War*, vol. 4, 472.

convincing Roosevelt to boost American war production. Lord Beaverbrook was instrumental in making the case and convincing the Americans that their own numbers needed to be increased dramatically. Indeed, his greatest achievement during the war was not as Minister of Aircraft Production, but in persuading the Americans to increase their production targets.[39] The Americans were stunned at how much Beaverbrook demanded they boost their production, which reinforced the views of the British that the Americans were naïve about the war effort, and reinforced American suspicions that the British were holding back their own production numbers.[40] For example, total American tank production for 1942 was 30,000, while the Germans threw that same number of tanks at the Russians that year. Beaverbrook wanted US production raised at least to 45,000. Bercuson and Holwig summarize the situation:

> He literally demanded a complete overhaul of American production methods and management . . . . In fact, no issue provoked more heated debate during ARCADIA than that of war production and allocation. It was political to the core. It aroused suspicions on both sides that each side was holding back production figures and allocation plans from one another. It was the only issue debated along purely nationalistic lines, American and British.[41]

When Roosevelt called for large production increases in his State of the Union Address at the end of January 1942, Churchill credited Beaverbrook and Hopkins for having convinced him.[42]

The responses of Roosevelt and Marshall to the British loss at Tobruk at Churchill's later visit to Washington in June also made a strong mark on their friendship. The loss was devastating for the British and for Churchill personally. But Churchill describes their response when

---

39 Schneer, *Ministers at War: Winston Churchill and His War Cabinet*, 165.
40 Bercuson and Holwig, *One Christmas in Washington*, 210.
41 Ibid.
42 Bercuson and Holwig, *One Christmas in Washington*, 230.

they heard the news: "Nothing could exceed the sympathy and chivalry of my two friends. There were no reproaches; not an unkind word was spoken. 'What can we do to help?' asked Roosevelt."[43] Churchill asked for Sherman tanks and Roosevelt accepted, despite Marshall's protestations that the tanks were only then coming into production and they had already been marked for American troops. Yet Marshall too gave in. Churchill was greatly touched by this and claims the Americans were "better than their word" because the first shipments of engines for the tanks were sunk off the coast of Bermuda and without being asked, Marshall supplied another fast ship for another supply of engines. The American donation of the tanks and of guns meant the British would have a two-to-one advantage of armor at the Battle of Alamein, the decisive battle of the war in Africa, and also the battle that Churchill claims served as the "hinge of fate": "It may almost be said, 'Before Alamein we never had a victory. After Alamein we never had a defeat.'"[44] Of the American donation, Churchill concluded, "A friend in need is a friend indeed."[45]

Marrakesh: Sunaisthesis at Sunset

Churchill's meeting with Roosevelt at Teheran was perhaps the low point of their friendship, where the demands of realpolitik exerted their greatest pressure on their bonds of affection. Churchill's visits to Washington were more of an equitable blend of "living together and sharing conversation and thinking" with the work of realpolitik. During their visit to Marrakesh, which concluded their Casablanca meeting in January 1943, they shared a moment of contemplation of beauty in beholding the sunset over the Atlas Mountains. Churchill told Roosevelt: "I must be with you when you see the sunset on the snows of the Atlas Mountains."[46] There they shared what Aristotle calls a joint perception of the good, the consummate act of virtue friendship:

43   Churchill, *The Second World War*, vol. 4, 344.
44   Ibid., 541.
45   Ibid., 344.
46   Ibid., 621.

But one's being is choice-worthy on account of the awareness of oneself as being good, and such an awareness is pleasant in itself. Therefore one also ought to share in a friend's awareness that he *is* (or share his friend's consciousness of his existence (*sunaisthanesthai hoti estin*)), and this would come through living together and sharing conversation and thinking; for this would seem to be what living together means in the case of human beings.[47]

This act of joint intellectual perception—"sunaisthesis" in Aristotle's Greek—is the capstone of friendship. It is the end to which the endeavors of individuals, including statesmen, point. Churchill frequently speaks of the capacity of Roosevelt, Marshall, Marlborough and other statesmen he admires to have a vision of the whole world situation, or "the whole military scene," as he sometimes phrased it. Their viewpoint is synoptic, and their vision is facilitated, enhanced, and even made possible by friendship with one who also has that capacity for synoptic vision of the whole situation. This is also how he describes Marlborough's friendship with Eugene of Savoy, as "two bodies with one soul" "working like two lobes of the same brain."[48]

More than that vision of affairs though, Churchill seemed to regard the capacity for philosophical vision, or at least vision of the true and the beautiful, more important and, indeed, more needful of a statesman. He describes his own activity of painting roughly in these terms:

> Painting is complete as distraction. I know of nothing which, without exhausting the body, more entirely absorbs the mind. Whatever the worries of the hour or the threats of the future, once the picture has begun to flow along, there is no room for them in the mental screen. They pass out into shadow and darkness. All one's mental light, such as it is, becomes concentrated on the task. Time stands respectfully aside, and it is only after many hesitations that luncheon knocks gruffly

47 Aristotle, *Nicomachean Ethics*, 1170b10–12.
48 Churchill, *Marlborough*, vol. 1, 775 and 825.

at the door . . . . The vain racket of the tourist gives place to the calm enjoyment of the philosopher.[49]

Churchill once visited Lick Observatory in California, and described observing the rings of planet and other celestial bodies. Martin Gilbert reports he told his wife: "After contemplating the heavens for some hours one wonders why one worries about the Epping Division."[50] This is the point where political and moral efforts lead—the *telos*, one might say. In Aristotelian terms, the exertions of political affairs only make sense when one has the capacity for leisurely philosophical contemplation.[51]

It is unclear what was going through the minds of Churchill and Roosevelt when they were contemplating the sunset at Marrakesh. They may not have been philosophizing. Even so, they seem to have been beholding some vision of the good and the noble, which was undoubtedly inspired by their joint affairs together and may even have given greater meaning to their shared efforts.

After they concluded their war planning business in Casablanca, Churchill insisted that he and Roosevelt drive an hour to Marrakesh, which was one of Churchill's favorite vacation spots. There they visited the residence of American Vice-Consul, Kenneth Pendar, the villa called La Sandia (also known as Villa Taylor, named after the American industrialist, Moses Taylor, who had it built in 1927).[52] Churchill and Pendar climbed to the top of the tower, and Churchill counted the number of steps—60—on the descent. At Churchill's behest, Roosevelt allowed two men to carry him up the stairs to see the view. Churchill's doctor, Moran, described Roosevelt being carried up to the rooftop: "his paralyzed legs dangling like the limbs of a ventriloquist's dummy, limp and flaccid."[53] Allowing himself to be handled in this way, when he normally went to great lengths to hide his disability, signifies no small amount of trust

49 Churchill, "Painting as a Pastime," *Thoughts and Adventures*, 318–19.
50 Martin Gilbert, *Winston S. Churchill*, vol. 5, 346. See Muller, "Introduction" in Churchill, *Thoughts and Adventures*, xxxiii.
51 See my *Friendship is the Form of Politics*, Chapters One and Two.
52 Meacham, *Franklin and Winston*, 210 and Roberts, *Masters and Commanders*, 347.
53 Roberts, *Masters and Commanders*, 347, citing an unidentified witness.

and fondness for Churchill. Churchill stated, "It's the most lovely spot in the whole world." Roosevelt agreed, later describing the view as "the most breathtakingly beautiful he had ever seen."[54] Inspector Thompson, one of the bodyguards, observed "The whole scene was a riot of the colour from which he draws [Churchill's] inspiration."[55] Meacham describes Pendar's description of the moment as "mystical":

> Never have I seen the sun set on those snow-capped peaks with such magnificence . . . . There had evidently been snow storms recently in the mountains, for they were white almost to their base, and looked more wild and rugged than ever, their sheer walls rising some 12,000 feet before use. The range runs more or less from east to west, and the setting sun over the palm oasis to our right shed a pink light on the snowy flank of the mountains. With the clear air, and the snow on the range, it looked near enough for us to reach out and touch its magnificence.[56]

After a while of maintaining this intellectual triangle of both beholding the sunset, of Churchill beholding Roosevelt, and perhaps of Roosevelt beholding Churchill, Churchill put Roosevelt's coat around his shoulders. Costigliola thinks Roosevelt regarded Churchill's placement of the cloak as an act of homage, consistent with him later telling Pendar, "I am the Pasha, you may kiss my hand."[57] However, this is too simplistic. Having suffered being carried up the steps, which at best would have been an aping of a Pasha being carried by his servants, Roosevelt undoubtedly felt a little embarrassed and likely would have tried regaining some face among his peers. Again, that he allowed himself to be carried and have his disability put on such display is a sign of remarkable trust and affection for Churchill.

54 Costigliola, *Roosevelt's Lost Alliances*, 182, citing Moran, *Churchill at War*, 99 (both quotations).
55 David Coombs, *Winston Churchill's Life Through His Paintings*, 163.
56 Meacham, *Franklin and Winston*, 210, citing Kenneth Pendar, *Adventure in Diplomacy*, 144–47.
57 Costigliola, *Roosevelt's Lost Alliances*, 182.

The group concluded the evening with "a very jolly dinner, about fifteen or sixteen, and we all sang songs. I sang, and the President joined in the choruses, and at one moment was about to try a solo. However, someone interrupted and I never heard this."[58] Choruses complemented the joint contemplation of the good.

Upon seeing off Roosevelt at the airport the next day as his friend commenced his long journey home, Churchill said, "He is the truest friend; he has the farthest vision; he is the greatest man I've ever known."[59] They had shared this "farthest vision" together. Churchill makes a point of describing how, after seeing off Roosevelt, he painted his only painting during the war from that same tower. He subsequently gave the painting, named "The Tower of Katoubia Mosque," to Roosevelt.[60] The painting completed their shared vision.

58 Churchill, *The Second World War*, vol. 4, 695.
59 Meacham, *Franklin and Winston*, 213.
60 Churchill, *The Second World War*, vol. 4, 622, and Roberts, *Masters and Commanders*, 347.

Part Three
The Friendly Regime

Chapter Six
Friendly Parliamentarians

Parliamentary Democracy
and the Problem of Political Greatness

Born in his ancestral home of Blenheim Palace, built by John Churchill the Duke of Marlborough, and son of Lord and Lady Randolph Churchill, Winston Churchill's background is hardly that of a "man of the people." Thus one may not be inclined to see him as a faithful exponent or representative of parliamentary democracy.

However, Churchill was to the end a servant of Parliament and his conduct as a statesman was imbued by the standards and habits of parliamentary democracy in such a way that can give us guidance today. In our day when concerns are expressed throughout Western democracies that prime ministers and presidents have gathered up extensive executive power at the expense of legislators, members of cabinet, Members of Parliament, and backbenchers, it is noteworthy to consider the following facts of Churchill's parliamentary career.

Churchill was a member of the British House of Commons for a total of 64 years between 1900 and 1964. He considered it his home. He represented five constituencies during that period. He served under thirteen Prime Ministers (Lord Salisbury, Balfour, Campbell-Bannerman, Asquith, Lloyd George, Bonar Law, Baldwin, MacDonald, Chamberlain, Attlee, Eden, Macmillan and Douglas-Home), and served two terms as Prime Minister himself (three if you count the Conservative government he led after the election call of 1945). Including Prime Minister, he held twelve different political offices. He served six sovereigns, spanning from Queen Victoria to Queen Elizabeth II.

From 1940 to 1945, Churchill led not just a party government, but a national government that included Conservative and Labour members (until the election call in 1945). Clement Atlee, the leader of the Labour Party, was a member of his War Cabinet. He always sought permission from King George VI and his War Cabinet for his trips to meet other leaders, which were numerous. Indeed he and King George seemed to enjoy a respectful and collaborative relationship.[1] Churchill faced and defeated overwhelmingly a vote of confidence in 1942 as well as a vote of censure that same year. While awaiting the results of the June 1945 election, he brought Clement Atlee, his opponent in that election and Leader of the Opposition at the time, to the Potsdam conference. He wanted Atlee to meet the other world leaders and familiarize himself better with the issues of the war, in case Churchill lost the election. Finally, Churchill indeed lost that election and became Leader of the Opposition.

Churchill lost the election in his own "finest hour" after he had led Great Britain and the Allied powers to victory over Germany, and just before victory over Japan. His description of these events conclude the sixth and final volume of *The Second World War*. The final paragraph of the work reprints his concession speech in which he reflects upon the war and concedes defeat to Labour. He concludes it by stating that he has submitted to the will of the people, for whom he is its "servant."[2] "Servant" is the final word of the *Second World War*. Thus parliamentary democracy controlled his political career in a way that, as he told Roosevelt and Stalin in Teheran in 1943, their respective political systems could not control theirs. He was the only one of the three whom the people he governed could immediately dismiss from office, and so they did in July 1945.[3]

When Churchill lost the election and left the grand stage, his powers and prestige were greater than those of his ancestor, the Duke of Marlborough, who lived before parliamentary supremacy. Marlborough led the command of his alliance but he depended upon his friend Godolphin

---

1   For details, see Kenneth Weisbrode, *Churchill and the King*.
2   Churchill, *The Second World War*, vol. 6, 584.
3   Ibid., 340–01.

to run the Exchequer, and upon the not always reliable Robert Harley to manage parliamentary support for his endeavors.

Churchill describes Marlborough's fall from power, brought about ultimately by his estranged friend Queen Anne, as the fall of the great man whose power and prestige, especially among the English population, threatened that of the Queen. Queen Anne and her court, along with Marlborough's enemies, painted him as a "second Cromwell" whom they chained down, "like a weary, baited bear chained to the post."[4] In Churchill's judgment, their fear of the great man led them to "violate the whole structure of personal and international good faith, of which British governments have so often prided themselves on being the architects and defenders."[5] He reports that Louis XIV rejoiced and was relieved at Marlborough's removal because, he allegedly claimed, "displacing the Duke of Marlborough will do for us what we desire."[6] The fear that Marlborough's contemporaries in Great Britain had of his greatness led them to commit the greatest treachery in bringing him down: "Nothing in the history of civilized peoples has surpassed this black treachery."[7]

If Marlborough was more powerful than the feared Cromwell, it may be said that Churchill's power was greater than even that of Marlborough. While Marlborough depended upon the favor of the Queen as well as the support of Parliament, of which he was not a sitting member, Churchill exercised vast executive power in place of King George VI; he was leader of his party in the House of Commons, he was Prime Minister, and he was Minister of Defense. Indeed, one of the reasons he was chosen Prime Minister instead of Lord Halifax is that the latter sat in the House of Lords and thereby would not be able to command a government.

Yet, when describing his assumption of office, Churchill explains, with reference to Napoleon's comment regarding the advantage of "short

---

4   Churchill, *Marlborough*, vol. 2, 784. See ibid., 734 and 766, for the comparisons with Cromwell. Churchill claims Marlborough, "at the head of armies and of the Great Alliance, was far greater in power than Cromwell before he became Lord Protector" (ibid., 766).
5   Ibid., 885.
6   Ibid., 913.
7   Ibid., 945.

and obscure" constitutions, that his "undefined" and "very wide powers" required "no legal or constitutional change."[8] Elsewhere he explains that in wartime, military and political leadership are one and the same: "It is not possible in a major war to divide military from political affairs. At the summit they are one."[9] Not in name but probably in fact Churchill was king during the war. However, unlike Marlborough, he declined when Queen Elizabeth offered to make him a duke. He was the "great man," the man of "superlative virtue," or a "classical prince," on whom the British bestowed considerable power and trust to lead the war effort.[10] More than Churchill's socio-economic status, this central factor must be addressed when understanding his stature as a parliamentarian.

But Churchill knew the fate of national saviours from his reading of history, and especially from his study of Marlborough. He also knew the ways nations destroy themselves in ridding themselves of their saviours. Despite its commitment to equality, parliamentary democracy, or responsible government, is the system of government best suited to avoid those problems because it is the one that best sustains political friendship, of which he was its great practitioner. He observes in his biography of Marlborough that great power was the cause of his downfall: "The pursuit of power with the capacity and in the desire to exercise it worthily is among the noblest of human occupations. But Power is a goddess who admits no rival in her loves."[11] Churchill knew the importance of sharing power, as well as the importance of letting people see one share power.

Churchill was a full-throated parliamentarian and defender of parliamentary government. He was also a "classical prince" whose command pushes the boundaries of parliamentary government. His

8   Ibid., 15–16.
9   Churchill, *The Second World War*, vol. 3, 24.
10   For a conceptual overview of this self-understanding of the creative "classical prince," see Tilo Schabert, "A Classical Prince." For "superlative virtue" and the problems such an individual has for a political regime where the multitude makes a competing claim for virtue, see Aristotle, *Politics*, 1284a1–1284b1, where he says, "such persons can no longer be regarded as a part of the city" (*Politics*, 1284a8). For discussion, see Waller Newell, *Tyranny: A New Interpretation*, 141–80.
11   Churchill, *Marlborough*, vol. 1, 919.

admiration for great statesmen and military leaders, like Napoleon, as well as his defense of the British Empire, simultaneously contradicts his devotion to parliamentary democracy and fits with it. For him, politics at its best is the domain of great statesmen equipped with genius. Yet such geniuses have to be friendly not merely to avoid the envy of fellow-citizens, but also to perfect the political art. The "classical prince" is also a friendly prince. This is the tension within magnanimity we saw in previous chapters, and now makes itself felt in his defense of parliamentary government as a form of political friendship.

Parliamentary Government: Government of Rules but Also of Persons

Friendship is not typically seen as central to Churchill's understanding of parliamentary or liberal democracy. His descriptions of the regime tend to highlight the formal aspects of liberal democracy and not the personal elements of political rule that more characterized premodern or aristocratic regimes like that of Great Britain after the rise of responsible government in the nineteenth century. However, closer scrutiny of some of his key statements concerning the moral goods associated with liberal democracy suggest that personal and political friendship do indeed play a critical role in its constitution, because they are part of the essential art of politics.[12]

In describing the moral and political hazards the Duke of Marlborough had to navigate, Churchill distinguishes the difference between politics in the early eighteenth century and that of the later nineteenth and twentieth centuries. He distinguishes the personalist politics of the

12 One should not be surprised to see a statesman, or classical prince, like Churchill regard the importance of so-called "informal" patterns of parliamentary democracy. The informal "party of friends" is a constant for the practice of politics, be it located in ancient Rome, Renaissance Florence, seventeenth-century England, or in 1970s Boston or 1980s world diplomacy: "the city entered into another 'history'—the 'history' of societies where the art of organizing a personal party, that is a party of 'friends,' has been shown to be the essential art of politics." (Schabert, *Boston Politics*, 102–03 and Heyking, "Friendship as Precondition," 87).

British monarchy and aristocracy of the earlier age from the modern parliamentary one, which contains fewer hazards than those faced by Marlborough:

> But in the days when party leaders were rival kings, when dislike of bad government was disloyalty, when resistance to a misguided king was treason, the ordinary transactions of modern political life wore a dire and sinister aspect. It was not possible to take part in public affairs without giving solemn oaths, nor to address the royal personage who was party leader except in the obsequious and adulatory terms which are still conventional. Not merely exclusion from public office, but confiscation of goods, imprisonment, and possibly death overhung all who were found on the losing side in any of the convulsions of State. In consequence public men often endeavored when possible to minimize their risks and to mitigate change. No such anxieties beset the Victorians or trouble us today. All our fundamentals have been for many generations securely established. The prizes of public life have diminished; its risks have been almost entirely removed. High office now means not the road to riches, but in most cases financial sacrifice. Power under the Crown passes from hand to hand with smooth decorum. The "Ins" and "Outs" take their turn in His Majesty's Government and in His Majesty's Opposition usually without a thought of personal vengeance, and often without a ruffle of private friendship.[13]

In the earlier age when politics was personal, political life was more hazardous because political friendship was identified with virtue-friendship. One risked one's life objecting to policy because opposition was seen as betrayal of one's person and thus the nation. Less so under responsible government, where authority is less personal and ostensibly more abstract because now it is lodged in institutions instead of the person of the monarch. Parliamentary or liberal democracy lowers the temperature

13 Churchill, *Marlborough*, vol. 1, 298–99.

of politics. His understanding of this point is essentially the same made by James Madison, who followed many thinkers since the inauguration of party government with the Settlement of 1688.[14] This is true for Great Britain under responsible government even though it is a monarchy. But now the monarchy avoids directly ruling and the Cabinet is composed of elected members. Legal authority replaces personal authority. Politics appears to be ruled by procedure and law, not by persons.

Parliamentary Democracy and Friendship of Persons: The Blend of the Formal and Informal

Churchill's understanding of the problem of friendship in responsible government does not stop at what seems to be its removal from the political sphere. In fact, the problem of friendship and its relationship to political practice deepens in important ways. We saw in Chapter One Churchill's view that parliamentary democracy, more so than other types of regime, requires moral practices like friendships, including those embodied by the "Other Club," because its very working is predicated not only on laws and parliamentary procedures, but on the moral virtues of civility and of course friendship.[15]

Indeed, one of Churchill's most famous statements on the subject is his description of the dramatic meeting he had with Neville Chamberlain and Lord Halifax, where they agreed that Churchill would replace Chamberlain as Prime Minister: "On this the momentous conversation came to an end, and we reverted to our ordinary easy and familiar manners of men who had worked for years together and whose lives in and out of office had been spent in all the friendliness of British politics."[16] Churchill credits the capacity of these parliamentarians to transfer power, in time of national emergency, to "the friendliness of British politics," and the capacity of parliamentarians, even with proverbial swords out,

---

14 For details on the origins of party government, see Harvey C. Mansfield, Jr., "Party Government and the Settlement of 1688," 933–46.

15 Martin Gilbert, *Churchill's Political Philosophy*, 101–02. See also Gilbert, *Will of the People*, 47–48.

16 Churchill, *The Second World War*, vol. 1, 598.

to conduct themselves cordially. While Chamberlain and Halifax both seemed to expect Churchill to fail as Prime Minister, he seemed to know them not simply as rivals and colleagues, but also as friends.[17]

As we saw in Chapter One: "An essential part of Churchill's political philosophy was his belief that nothing, even in the bitterest of political controversies, must be allowed to damage the fabric of the society as a whole. It was his strong conviction that within the democratic system political disagreements, whether inside or across party, must not entail personal animosities. Such animosities would, he believed, themselves endanger the democratic process."[18] Parliamentary democracy is governed by rules and procedures, but something like political friendship is required on top of that to sustain the regime because rules and procedures alone cannot do it.

In fact, Gilbert demonstrates that it was Churchill's enduring practice of friendships with numerous people that enabled him to be a successful statesman and parliamentarian. For example, he points out that in May 1940, relations between Tories and Labour were at their most bitter: "it was Churchill under whom the Labour Party was willing to serve. And it was Churchill who then brought the leading figures of the Labour movement into central positions of war policy and war direction."[19] They outright refused to serve under Chamberlain in a national government because, among many other reasons, he "did not invite friendship or confidences" and was contemptuous toward opponents.[20]

Churchill's ability to practice friendship with fellow parliamentarians, including those in other parties, was crucial, since Churchill needed Labour's support, and their support among the major labour unions, in order to achieve the production goals for war equipment that Great Britain so desperately needed. Churchill's friendships with Cabinet

17 Schneer, *Ministers at War*, 32.
18 Gilbert, *Churchill's Political Philosophy*, 101–02.
19 Ibid. Schneer explains how Churchill's neglect of the Beveridge Report, championed by Labour, eroded his domestic support and played a factor in losing in the 1945 election (Schneer, *Ministers at War*, chs. 10–12).
20 Schneer, *Ministers at War*, 12–13. Schneer describes how Chamberlain pathetically appealed to his "friends" in Parliament for the vote of confidence, only to find himself with very few.

ministers also enabled them to befriend one another. Churchill became good friends with his Labour colleagues, especially Clement Atlee, throughout the war.[21] Further, Dilks credits these friendships, the "loyalty and the excellence of the administrative machine," for keeping the government together during Churchill's considerable absences during the war.[22] We saw previously how his friendship with Roosevelt served as a model for the two leaders' staffs to work together and, in key instances, to befriend one another. In other words, Churchill's capacity to create not merely a party government but a national government with an effective administration during the war was based to a large degree on his personal friendships with numerous key figures.

Gilbert shows how this worked. Churchill's strategy was the same as when he and his good friend F. E. Smith founded the "Other Club" as a forum in which to practice convivium in a way that transcended political and partisan affiliation and concern: "The Club survived. So too did Churchill's continual efforts to maintain civility, and friendship, with political critics and opponents. 'I am confident', he had once written to one fellow Cabinet Minister, 'that our friendship will never be even ruffled by the incidental divergence of honest opinion inseparable from the perplexities of politics and affairs'. This attitude included the Labour Party leaders against whom he argued so fiercely in the 1920s."[23]

Churchill strove to make gestures of civility and friendship with fellow parliamentarians, including those opposing him when they formed government:

> When the first Labour Government came to office January 1924, Churchill at once sent Ramsay MacDonald a letter of friendship and encouragement. MacDonald replied: "No letter received by me at this time has given me more pleasure than yours. I wish we did not disagree so much!—but there

21 Ibid., 228.
22 Dilks, *Churchill and Company*, 54. Eden grew to love Churchill and "that emotion survived all tempests" (ibid., 55).
23 Gilbert, *Churchill's Political Philosophy*, 101, citing letter of September 7, 1908, to R. B. Haldane.

it is. In any event I hope your feelings are like mine. I have always held you personally in much esteem, & I hope, whatever fortune may have in store for us, that personal relationship will never be broken. Perhaps I may come across you occasionally."[24]

Gilbert documents other cases of the good relations Churchill kept with Labour MPs, even when he was one of their fiercest critics. It was no mere public pose:

> In private, Labour men knew that they could turn to him if they were in difficulties. After the death of Philip Snowden, his widow, a former suffragette and dedicated socialist, wrote to Churchill: Your generosity to a political opponent marks you forever in my eyes the 'great gentleman' I have always thought you. Had I been in trouble which I could not control myself, there is none to whom I should have felt I could come with more confidence that I should be gently treated.[25]

Gilbert shows how Churchill wielded his friendships to assemble coalitions during crisis situations during the 1920s, which paid off for him later, most notably with the 1940 War Cabinet. This is not to say that Churchill was never tough, manipulative, or Machiavellian with political allies and rivals, including Beaverbrook and Eden, who had their own leadership ambitions with which he had to contend and ultimately swat away.[26] Even so, he understood the importance of friendships for opening up moral and political spaces for statesmen to work in, especially during times of crisis whereby previously earned trust and goodwill enables cross-partisan cooperation. In these ways informal practices sustain and even enhance the formal procedures of Parliament. We turn

24 Ibid., citing letter of January 27, 1924.
25 Ibid., 101.
26 For details on how Churchill managed his War Cabinet, oftentimes in a somewhat Machiavellian manner, see Jonathan Schneer, *Ministers at War: Winston Churchill and His War Cabinet* and Roger Hermiston, *All Behind You, Winston: Churchill's Great Coalition, 1940–45*.

now to the workings of those formal procedures as an expression of political friendship.

Parliament as Political Friendship

Churchill's 1909 statement that "democracy properly understood means the association of all through the leadership of the best," certainly reflects his view that Parliament is the central institution of Great Britain and perhaps that a privileged few are more suitable for ruling than the many.[27] He held the nineteenth-century view of Parliament as a social club where everyone knew one another. But one cannot press the charge of elitism of this view too far because, for Churchill, Parliament expresses the people's will and derives its authority through elections: "It is not Parliament that should rule; it is the people who should rule through Parliament."[28] As a Liberal and friend of Lloyd George, Churchill's criticisms of the British aristocracy suggest he was no sympathizer with the aristocratic form of rule which presupposes the equation of hereditary rule with talent.[29] At times he showed acidic contempt for Britain's political elites, as in his speech at Horsham, July 23, 1936: "I can well imagine some circles of smart society, some groups of wealthy financiers, and the elements in this country which are attracted by the idea of a Government strong enough to keep the working classes in order; people who hate democracy and freedom, I can well imagine such people accommodating themselves fairly easily to Nazi domination."[30] But nor was he a radical democrat. While he expressed fears that mass democracy would degenerate into a form of despotism, he admired democracy's ability to raise up new leaders from the middle class, including Gladstone, Disraeli, Lloyd George, Bonar

27 Kevin Theakston, "'Part of the Constitution': Winston S. Churchill and Parliamentary Democracy," 31, citing *Complete Speeches*, II, 1424.
28 Churchill to House of Commons, November 11, 1947, quoted in Gilbert, *Will of the People*, 124.
29 Churchill, "The Upkeep of the Aristocracy," 37–38 (dated December 17, 1909).
30 Churchill, speech at Horsham, July 23, 1936, quoted by Gilbert, *Churchill's Political Philosophy*, 97.

Law, and Chamberlain.[31] He was a parliamentarian who thought Parliament, while elected, also leads the country and its membership must be composed of the best individuals of that country. Churchill evidently thought the elites or the "ruling classes" of any society have the power to influence and shape it, for good or for ill, and oftentimes despite their intentions.[32]

Parliament and responsible government in general must balance all the viewpoints of society: "It was always found in the past to be a misfortune to a country when it was governed from one particular point of view, or in the interests of any particular class, whether it was the Court or the Church, or the Army or the mercantile or labouring classes. Every country ought to be governed from some central view, where all classes and all interests are proportionately represented."[33] This looks less like aristocracy than it does roughly what Aristotle calls polity, whose "central view" Aristotle alludes to by calling it a middling regime whereby the different factions in society balance one another out under rule of law.[34] Its modern version is parliamentary democracy, or responsible government.

Parliament represents the life of the nation: one finds "by far the closest association yet achieved between the life of the people and the action of the state."[35] In parliamentary democracy, the head and the body of the state, the will of the people and their agent(s), were the most closely combined of any political regime so far enacted. Churchill describes this "close association" in British political life in *My Early Life*:

> Our wise and prudent law spread a general election over nearly six weeks. Instead of all our electors voting blindly on one day, and only learning next morning what they had done,

31 Theakston, *Winston Churchill and the British Constitution*, 2.
32 Churchill, *A History of the English-Speaking Peoples*, vol. 1, 231; Havers, *Leo Strauss and Anglo-American Democracy*, 117.
33 Churchill to House of Commons, July 29, 1903, quoted in Gilbert, *Will of People*, 31.
34 See Aristotle, *Politics*, 1329b35, and III.11.
35 Churchill, "Parliamentary Government and the Economic Problem," *Thoughts and Adventures,* 247; see Gilbert, *Will of the People*, 74.

national issues were really fought out. A rough but earnest and searching national discussion took place in which leading men on both sides played part. The electorate of a constituency was not unmanageable in numbers. A candidate could address all his supporters who wished to hear him. A great speech by an eminent personage would often turn a constituency or even a city. Speeches of well-known and experienced statesmen were fully reported in all the newspapers and studied by wide political classes. Thus by a process of rugged argument the national decision was reached in measured steps.[36]

It may be the case that Churchill thought this description no longer applied by the 1930s, when he wrote "Parliamentary Government and the Economic Problem." There he expresses doubts that Parliament was prepared to handle the economic problems of the Great Depression, and that mass democracy had made society into a "fluid mass distracted by newspapers" preferring titillation from controversies to actual speeches, debate, and deliberation.[37] Even so, by alluding to this higher standard in this essay he indicates how he regarded it as the standard to which to aspire.

The amazing thing about Parliament is that in it, its highest ministers of state are "questioned and cross-questioned on every conceivable subject and entering into the whole process with *respect and with good will*."[38] It is government by talking, not by fisticuffs.[39] It entails "'talking

36 Churchill, *My Early Life: A Roving Commission*, 370–71. See James Muller, "Churchill's Understanding of Politics," 295.

37 Churchill, *My Early Life: A Roving Commission*, 370–73. See Muller, "Churchill's Understanding of Politics," 296.

38 Churchill, "Is Parliament Merely a Talking Shop?" *Daily Mail*, 17 April 1935, cited by Gilbert, *Will of the People*, 83. Emphasis added.

39 Churchill to House of Commons, 6 June 1951: "The object of Parliament is to substitute for fisticuffs" (quoted in Gilbert, *Will of the People*, 134). See also Churchill, *Thoughts and Adventures*, xxi, 245. Churchill seems to have gotten this phrase from Macaulay (Theakston, *Winston Churchill and the British Constitution*, 1).

by the responsible representatives of great constituencies who meet each other *face to face*' and who debate issues in a serious manner far from 'the raucous caucus clamour' of popular elections."[40] Government by talking is "an assemblage of persons who represent, or who claim to represent, the nation, meet together face to face, and argue out our affairs. The public at large having perforce chosen these persons from among those who were put before them, submits itself in spite of some misgivings and repinings to their judgment."[41] While parliamentarians are members of their respective parties, "the parliamentary conception is still dominant."[42] They are parliamentarians first, party members second.

Further, "The only foundation for good government and happy results for the people is a *high standard of comradeship and fellowship* between those who are called upon to handle their affairs."[43] Churchill points out that Parliament's "long tradition, its collective personality, its flexible procedure, *its social life*, its unwritten inviolable conventions have made an organism more effective for the purpose of assimilation than any of which there is record."[44] The terms I have emphasized in these quotations suggest the role played by the moral virtues in parliamentary democracy. Notice he states the "only foundation" for good government is "comradeship and fellowship." He does not mention other contenders for such a foundation, including law.

Members of Parliament indeed form a club, as Churchill considered his parliamentary friends his best friends, or at least as his fellow lifelong club members: "Legislation and the governance of Britain were his constant companions, the objects of his persistent work and evolving

---

40   Kevin Theakston, *Winston Churchill and the British Constitution*, (London: Politico's, 2004), 1–2, quoting a speech of 1923, reprinted in *Complete Speeches*, IV, 3394. Emphasis added.

41   Churchill, "Parliamentary Government and the Economic Problem," *Thoughts and Adventures*, 245.

42   Ibid., 246.

43   Gilbert, *Will of the People*, 96, citing Churchill, in *News of the World*, January 1, 1939. Emphasis added.

44   Churchill "Parliamentary Government and the Economic Problem," *Thoughts and Adventures*, 248. Emphasis added.

expertise. Elections and electioneering were part of his life-blood. His fellow parliamentarians were among his closest, lifelong friends."[45] Parliament as the head of the nation is also bound together by "comradeship and fellowship" and "respect and good will" by individuals who "meet each other face to face." They represent their constituencies and viewpoints to be sure, but they also face one another as moral and self-governing agents responsible for their actions, as individual members, and as a body.

For these reasons, Churchill regarded the architecture of the House as important. Its oblong shape and its small size contribute to giving its members a sense of responsibility for their actions, and also enables a conversational manner to take place. He writes:

> Its shape should be oblong and not semicircular. Here is a very potent factor in our political life. The semicircular assembly, which appeals to political theorists, enables every individual or every group to move round the centre, adopting various shades of pink according as the weather changes. I am a convinced supporter of the party system in preference to the group system . . . . It is easy for an individual to move through those insensible gradations from Left to Right, but the act of crossing the Floor is one which requires serious consideration. I am well informed on this matter, for I have accomplished that difficult process, not only once, but twice.[46]

Regarding his twice having crossed the floor, Churchill allegedly quipped after re-joining the Conservatives in 1924, "Anyone can rat, but

---

45 Gilbert, *Will of the People*, 2–3.
46 Churchill, *The Second World War*, vol. 4, 150. Churchill continues by contrasting the wisdom of custom, which produced the design of the British House of Commons, with logic, which, "a poor guide as compared with custom," has created those semi-circular assemblies. See also his speech, "Speech on Rebuilding the House of Commons (1943)," in *Conservatism: An Anthology of Social and Political Thought from David Hume to the Present*, 285–89.

it takes a certain amount of ingenuity to re-rat." Parliamentary democracy must promote among its practitioners a strong sense of personal responsibility for one's actions. The pattern of government versus opposition, by providing a stark contrast of options and opinions, is meant not only to do that among parliamentarians, but to make it easier for citizens to see their parliamentarians exercising responsibility. This process goes on within the customary framework of parliamentarians viewing themselves first and foremost as members of the House, and members of their parties after that.[47] Indeed, Churchill thought "crossing the floor of the House" was the ultimate assertion of the freedom of an individual Member of Parliament.[48]

The size of the House of Commons should also promote that sense of responsibility as well as conversation among parliamentarians. Churchill emphasizes that the House should:

> [N]ot be big enough to contain all its members at once without overcrowding, and that there should be no question of every member having a separate seat reserved for him .
> . . . If the House is big enough to contains all its members nine-tenths of its debates will be conducted in the depressing atmosphere of an almost empty or half-empty chamber. The essence of good House of Commons speaking is the conversational style, the facility for quick, informal interruptions and interchanges. Harangues from a rostrum would be a bad substitute for the conversational style in which so much of our business is done. But the conversational style requires a fairly small space, and there should be on great occasions a sense of crowd and urgency. There should be a sense of the importance of much that is said, and a sense that great matters are being decided, there and then, by the House.[49]

47 Churchill, "Parliamentary Government and the Economic Problem," *Thoughts and Adventures*, 246.
48 Gilbert, *Will of the People*, 32.
49 Churchill, *Second World War*, vol. 5, 150–51.

Elsewhere Churchill writes of the "crowd and urgency" of the House: "The essence of keen debate is the sense of a crowd, clustering together craning forward, gathering round the speaker, with the cheers and counter-cheers flung back from side to side."[50] Note however that this "crowd and urgency" is not the same as the "clamour" of the general election because the customs and procedures of the House of Commons "tames, calms, instructs, reconciles, and rallies" the various viewpoints and opinions stated there. In James Madison's words, parliamentary procedure gives the "mild voice of reason" the space to have itself heard, however dimly.[51]

Responsibility and conversation in the House of Commons express political friendship. Parliamentarians, as representatives of their ridings and as members of their respective parties, converse and debate and take collective responsibility for their decisions. Though there is of course partisan difference and contestation, there is also respect for the House, its procedures, customs, and history, as well as pride in office that they all share as parliamentarians. There is unity and difference in political friendship.

---

50 Theakston, *Winston Churchill and the British Constitution*, 136, quoting, Churchill, *News of the World*, 18 December 1938.

51 James Madison, Federalist No. 42, 219. See also my "Liberal Education Embedded in Civic Education for Responsible Government: The Case of John George Bourinot," 44–76.

Chapter Seven
Parliamentary Democracy and Empire

Parliamentary Democracy as Political Friendship

The responsibility practiced by parliamentarians enjoying comradeship and fellowship is reflected as well in the act of a citizen voting. Churchill however did not especially like elections, but he does see their special festive significance in bringing together the English polity: "As the reader may have gathered, I do not like elections, but it is in my many elections that I have learnt to know and honour the people of this island. They are good all through. Liberals, Tories, Radicals, Socialists, how much kindliness and good sportsmanship there is in all!"[1] While he did not seem to enjoy campaigning, he does seem to have recognized how an election is a kind of festival or sporting event that involves a high degree of play, whose spirit both facilitates strong competition among campaigners, but also a sense of solidarity of being participants in a larger significant game.

Churchill provides a more illuminating description of the essence of elections when he states:

> The foundation of all democracy is that the people have the right to vote. To deprive them of that right is to make a mockery of all the high-sounding phrases that are so often used. At the bottom of all the tributes paid to democracy is the little man, walking into the little booth, with a little pencil, making a little cross on a little bit of paper—no amount of rhetoric

---

1   Churchill, "Election Memories," *Thoughts and Adventures*, 218.

or voluminous discussion can possibly diminish the over-whelming importance of that point.[2]

Churchill describes the act of voting, though humble, as a moment of utmost civic responsibility. Whereas parliamentarians face each other and take responsibility for their own choices and for the actions of Parliament, the voter faces his moment of responsibility alone. Voting is about making a choice regarding who governs. By viewing the act of voting this way, Churchill understood an important distinction that modern political scientists frequently overlook. Modern political scientists and pollsters tend to conflate the act of voting with the preferences respondents register in polls.[3] People register their preferences when responding to polls; they make choices when voting. Polls register likes and dislikes, while voting is making a choice regarding who should govern. The difference is as fundamental as the difference between how one judge's a politician's position on an issue, and how one judges his character, or between one's opinion and one's moral ethos.[4] As Aristotle reminds us, our choices, not our opinions, form our ethos.

Churchill summarizes the ethic of self-government:

A high degree of personal freedom and a sense of lawful independence has certainly been the main characteristic not only of the British people but of the English-speaking races, now spread so widely through the world. Freedom of religion, freedom of thought, freedom of movement, freedom to choose or change employment; the inviolability even of the humblest home; the right and the power of the private citizen to appeal to impartial courts against the State of the day;

---

2   Churchill to Commons, Oct 31, 1944, quoted by Gilbert, *Will of the People*, 114.

3   See Harvey Mansfield, *America's Constitutional Soul*, 128–62.

4   I owe this insight to Ken Boessenkool and our many discussions over this and many other points regarding practical politics.

freedom of speech and writing; freedom of the Press; freedom of combination and agitation within the limits of long-established laws, of the right of regular opposition to Government; the power to turn out a Government and put another set of men in their places by lawful, constitutional means; and finally the sense of association with the State and of some responsibility for its actions and conduct.[5]

Parliamentary democracy entails the forms of liberty, which include voting and those listed here, but also the social habits of self-government that culminate in the "sense of association with the State and of some responsibility for its actions and conduct." The forms of liberty are complemented by the informalities and moral virtues of taking responsibility for oneself before others, face to face.

The "little man" with his pencil embodies the grand tradition of liberty of the English-speaking peoples, whose characteristic virtues not only sustain that liberty but also the solidarity together in the regime that secures liberty: "The chief characteristic of the British islander is a natural instinctive hatred of tyranny in any form—aristocratic, theocratic, plutocratic, bureaucratic, democratic, all forms are equally odious."[6] This hatred of tyranny gives them "a vigorous, active, law-making citizenship expressing itself through Parliament and especially through the House of Commons."[7] Democratic leaders owe their people candor. The people must practice a "considered, instructed, organized public opinion . . . . [C]itizens in every class" must make "ceaseless political exertion . . . in all parts of the country."[8] Their "hatred" and "vigor"—their *thumos*, to use an ancient Greek philosophical term—is moderate, for Churchill could also speak of the "ancient wisdom of the island" and the "wisdom

5   Churchill, "Are Parliaments Obsolete?" *Persons Magazine*, June 1934, 555–56.
6   Churchill, "Are Parliaments Obsolete?," *Pearson's Magazine*, June 1934. See Theakston, *Winston Churchill and the British Constitution*, 16.
7   Ibid.
8   Churchill, "Bolshevism and Imperial Sedition" November 4, 1920, in *Winston S. Churchill: His Complete Speeches*, vol. 3, 3026. See Arnn, *Churchill's Trial*, 225.

of our ancestors."[9] This synthesis of moderated *thumos* and wisdom or common sense is the basis for their self-government and political friendship.

Churchill's understanding of the common sense decency, toughness, and friendliness of the British people resembles Immanuel Kant's assessment of the Lithuanians, who he thought possessed the characteristics needed for self-government and political friendship: "He is farther from slavishness than the neighboring peoples, that he is used to talking with his superiors in a tone of equality and trusting frankness, which the superiors also do not mind nor coldly refuse a handshake, because they also find him consenting to everything that is fair."[10] Susan Shell observes that in Kant's description are the qualities of open-heartedness and trusting candor that "one is almost tempted to call civic friendship."[11]

These comments on Churchill's understanding of Parliament and the regime of parliamentary democracy qualify his famous statement, made first by someone else, now cliché, that "Democracy is the worst form of government, except for all those other forms that have been tried from time to time."[12] Usually this is taken to reflect Churchill's purported view that politics is at best a malign and dreary activity, and that human beings are advised to put up with the "least bad" form of democracy because aspiring to anything greater in politics leads inevitably to destruction. While moderation is a central political virtue, such a view is too low, and does not accurately reflect Churchill's understanding of parliamentary democracy as political friendship.

---

9 Churchill, "Are Parliaments Obsolete?" See Theakston, *Winston Churchill and the British Constitution*, 21.

10 Kant, "Postscript to Christian Gottlieb Mielcke's Lithuanian-German and German-Lithuanian Dictionary," 432.

11 Susan Shell, "'*Nachschrift eines Freundes*': Kant on Language, Friendship and the Concept of a People," 97. Though Churchill's and Kant's reflections run along the same lines, Kant's penetrate more deeply into the core of civic friendship. Kant's thinking on friendship is underappreciated. See my "'The Sum Total of Our Relationships to Others': Kant on Friendship," in *The Luminosity of Modernity: Essays on the Political Thought of David Walsh*.

12 Churchill to House of Commons, November 11, 1947.

Island Story as Political Friendship

Churchill frequently spoke of "our long story" or "our island story."[13] The history of Great Britain is not simply its events but truly and genuinely a story in which citizens and statesmen partook in the conflict and challenges that beset them together. Perhaps his most famous invocation of the "island story" was his speech to Cabinet in May 1940 where he convinced them Great Britain could not negotiate a separate peace with Hitler: "If this long island story of ours is to end at last, let it end only when each one of us lies choking in his own blood upon the ground."[14] The great "island story," which began with the great deeds and sacrifices of their ancestors, could never end with shameful surrender, but only with their deaths. Meacham suggests his "Finest Hour" broadcast also appeals to the "island story" because of its echoes of Shakespeare's Henry V before the Battle of Agincourt.[15]

The "island story" of Britons, and their common sense, is the expression of that civic friendship. Churchill seems to have learned the term from Tennyson: "Not once or twice in our rough island-story/ The path of duty was the way to glory."[16] For Churchill, the phrase summarizes the political friendship of Britons. A brief look at this symbol and his understanding of British history suggests he regarded Great Britain as enjoying a political friendship.

Theakston summarizes Churchill's view of the common sense of the Britons:

> He was strongly conscious also that it was a historical constitution, growing out of "the wisdom of our ancestors" and "the practice of former times" as he put it. Human societies

---

13 Meacham, *Franklin and Winston*, 169. See also, Jonathan Scott, "Introduction: Britain's Island Idea," in *When the Waves Ruled Britannia: Geography and Political Identities, 1500–1800*, 7–8.

14 Churchill, *The Churchill War Papers*, vol. 2, 182–84.

15 Meacham, *Franklin and Winston*, 169.

16 See Churchill, *The Second World War*, vol. 5, 146, citing "the famous lines" of "Ode to the Death of Duke of Wellington" by Lord Tennyson, 201–02, 209–10.

and institutions are not mechanical structures but organic ("plants that grow"), he believed. Systems of government express and grow out of and through a country's and a community's history, culture, and traditions. Thus to say that the British constitution was "mainly British common sense," as he did in 1908, was actually to affirm its reality and strength.[17]

The "island story" is Great Britain's historical lived experience of finding and securing liberty, whose utmost expression is in parliamentary democracy. It is a history of conflict to be sure, but one in which the islanders strove for common cause, of finding that "central view" that parliamentary democracy is meant to secure.

Churchill blended Burkean, Whiggish, and Bagehotian viewpoints in his understanding of the British constitution and its island story. He could see it in Whiggish terms, as a long struggle and march toward greater freedom and liberty. However, he did not think there was anything inevitable or preordained about this process. The achievements of civilization are always won by hard work and struggle, and can easily be lost. He could also understand the island story in terms of Walter Bagehot and his *English Constitution*, according to which the English constitution is in constant oscillation from social and political changes, but it always finds the center to maintain its equilibrium. But he could describe it also in Burkean "organic" terms to express how the island story is the aggregate of a myriad of decisions and actions made by individuals working in conflict and in concert. Churchill's admiration of the English constitution's venerability and flexibility echoes Burke's famous statement that the English constitution is a "partnership not only between those who are living, but between those who are living, those who are dead, and those who are to be born."[18] This view can also be seen in Churchill's description of "the central principles of civilisation" as "the subordination of the ruling authority to the settled customs of

---

17 Theakston, *Winston Churchill and the British Constitution*, 21.
18 Edmund Burke, *Reflections on the Revolution in France*, 193. See Arnn, *Churchill's Trial*, 218.

the people and to their will as expressed through the Constitution."[19] Political friendship is the precondition or even expression of a people enjoying "settled customs," and their "subordination of the ruling authority" presupposes their capacity to act in a unified manner, as expressed in the forms of their constitution. Theakston describes how the Whiggish, Bagehotian, and Burkean elements combine in Churchill's overall view:

> Churchill's sense of the British constitution drew upon themes and ideas that can be traced back to Burke, Macaulay and Bagehot. Like Burke, he emphasized the importance of historical continuity, inheritance, adaptation and preservation in the political system and political community. Like Macaulay, he believed that British history demonstrated that the constitution could peacefully assimilate and adapt to change while preserving its forms and traditions. The relationship between the different elements of the constitution might change over time, but the integrity of the structure would not be compromised. And like Bagehot, he understood the stabilizing and constraining functions of custom, tradition, ceremony and the theatrical aspects of the constitution—all helping the British constitution to absorb change.[20]

Whiggish liberty, Burkean inheritance, and Bagehotian equilibrium all presuppose a *sensus communis*, an unwritten constitution, on the part of the British people.

These elements express a political friendship, which Churchill at times could describe in terms very close to that of Aristotle, as when he explained that the constitution depends on a "union of consenting minds" "aiming at the same objective." Despite partisan differences, Britons must "feel the greatness and glory of Britain and the happiness of her

---

19 Churchill, "Civilisation," 5991.
20 Kevin Theakston, "'Part of the Constitution': Winston S. Churchill and Parliamentary Democracy," 34.

people have always been, and still are, the objective on which they are marching."[21]

"Island story" is a story in which individuals, including seemingly "great men" like Churchill or Marlborough, play a part: "No single generation is the owner of all that has been built up here during so many centuries. We are only the trustees and life-tenants, owing much to the past, and hoping . . . to do our duty by the future."[22] Each citizen forms part of each generation, which forms a chapter of the "island story." The emphasis is on how individuals form parts of a greater whole, not to be subsumed by that whole, but the whole is validated because it serves the liberties of its subjects.

The capacity to practice friendship as a story, where actions are completed in reflection and speech and where reflection and speech are themselves action, formed the basis of Churchill's understanding of Great Britain's "island story":

> In Churchill's cosmos there was joy in the journey; without darkness there could be no light. This was one reason he often spoke of "our long story" or "our island story"—stories require conflict and challenges, victories and defeats. He wanted a part in the battles of his time so that he would live in the legend of the ages, and he assumed others did, too. It was no coincidence that in his "Finest Hour" broadcast he tied the trials of the present to the collective consciousness of the world to come. Men will still say it was a call to arms reminiscent of Shakespeare's Henry V bracing his men to fight at Agincourt with the image of how the tale would be told from generation to generation.[23]

"Our island story" is not simply the story or history of Great Britain, for Great Britain *is* the "island story." The entity called "Great Britain" is

---

21 Churchill, "The Centre Party," July 15, 1919, in *Winston Churchill: His Complete Speeches*, vol. 3, 2815. See Arnn, *Churchill's Trial*, 225.

22 Churchill, "Whither Britain?" *Listener*, 17 January 1934. See Theakston, *Winston Churchill and the British Constitution*, 22–23.

23 Meacham, *Winston and Franklin*, 168–69.

the "island story" acted "from generation to generation." In the terms used by Plato's Athenian Stranger in the *Laws*, Great Britain as "island story" *is* the "*nomos*," the song sung by the dancing citizens: "Best of strangers . . . we ourselves are poets, who have to the best of our ability created a tragedy that is the most beautiful and the best; at any rate, our whole political regime is constructed as the imitation of the most beautiful and best way of life, which we at least assert to be really the truest tragedy . . . . We are your rivals as artists and performers of the most beautiful drama, which true law alone can by nature bring to perfection—as we hope."[24] Their "story" is their action, which in turn is their "story." Churchill, who "not only makes laws for his people but writes their songs as well, in the sense that his speeches are battle cries, dirges for the fallen and hymns of victory,"[25] viewed the "island story" or *nomos* of Great Britain in similar terms.

Empire and Friendship

The portrait painted in this chapter of Churchill the friendly parliamentarian has emphasized the manner in which parliamentary democracy encourages statesmen to act as partners with others in furthering their political objectives. We have seen how Churchill worked within the rules and procedures of parliamentary democracy to further the common good of Great Britain.

Churchill's devotion to parliamentary democracy is in some tension with his devotion to the empire, and to the greatness of the individual statesman. It contradicts his devotion to the empire because empire entails rule over others, and it seems too that empire depends upon rule by emperor, one who hardly shares rule as parliamentarians do.

Yet, his devotion to empire accords with his devotion to parliamentary democracy because, as the best type of political regime, it deserves to be glorified. As Aristotle says, glory is a proper accompaniment of virtue. Empire seems a natural extension of a nation's pride in itself and

24 Plato, *Laws,* 817b–c. For discussion, see my *The Form of Politics: Aristotle and Plato on Friendship*, chapter 6.
25 Malcolm Cowley, "Mr. Churchill Speaks," 537.

is an exercise in national self-glorification, something Churchill strove to pursue. Indeed, he seems to have thought imperial rule, especially over India, could improve the moral excellence of the British themselves.[26]

This is not the place to assess Churchill's attitude toward India or his general idea of empire. This has been done elsewhere.[27] Our purpose is simply to point out a tension between his commitment to empire and the importance he placed upon friendship for politics. It is a tension that has its roots in the manner in which the magnanimous man practices friendship, as discussed in Chapter Two.

Churchill regarded the benefits the British empire brought to its subjects as the result of its commitment to liberty and parliamentary democracy. For Churchill, the moral excellence of the empire was owed to the moral excellence of the parliamentary regime upon which it was based. If ruling shows the true measure of a (great) man, as Aristotle claims, Churchill thought empire a fitting exercise for the British: "the peculiar gifts for administration and civic virtue of our race may find a healthy and honourable scope,"[28] especially for citizens of Great Britain that had become more of a mass democracy offering fewer and fewer outlets for publicly spirited individuals at home. As Muller observes, "in the first decade of the twentieth century, Churchill foresaw a new start for Britain's poorest citizens in the empty lands of the colonial empire. Later, as Britons turned inward toward the private pursuit of security and well-being, Churchill saw in the empire a lingering chance for public careers and for public-minded citizenship, correcting the anonymous individualism of modern democracy."[29] Churchill saw empire as an antidote for the lack of constructive outlets at home for public-spirited citizens. Political life in the late nineteenth century was characterized by the "rough but earnest and searching national discussion"

26 Kirk Emmert, *Winston S. Churchill on Empire*, xiii.
27 Emmert, *Winston S. Churchill on Empire*; James, *Churchill and Empire*; Toye, *Churchill's Empire*; Arnn, *Churchill's Trial*, 97–116.
28 Churchill, *My African Journey*, quoted by Emmert, *Winston S. Churchill on Empire*, 60.
29 James Muller, "Review: Imperialism as the Highest Stage of Civilization," 582.

conducted by leaders and citizens. This robust political life had been replaced by "a fluid mass distracted by newspapers" by the 1920s and 1930s.[30] He came to see empire as a possible way to rejuvenate civic virtues, but it is unclear whether the "gifts of administration" empire was to revivify among the Britons were of the same quality as the deliberative virtues that enabled a "rough but earnest and searching national discussion."

He saw empire as a "fully civilizing activity."[31] I write these lines as the son of parents who were among the first Baltic-German immigrants to Canada after World War Two. Despite his role in the "largest forcible population transfer in human history," I am certain that the decency the British empire extended toward my parents and other Baltic-Germans far surpasses anything that any other empire in human history has accorded its former enemies (victims of the famine in British East India during World War Two may have reason to see things otherwise).[32]

Even so, Churchill was well aware of the evils of imperial rule toward its subjects, but also towards the imperialists. He wrote extensively about the atrocities British authorities committed against the Sudanese and others, the result, he seemed to think, of benevolent imperialists having to adopt the methods of barbarians themselves in order to defeat them. He also recognized that imperialists could act even more wickedly than barbarians because their own "moral sadism" convinces them that their allegedly superior morality makes their acts of brutality truly

---

30 Churchill, *My Early Life*, 370–72, cited by Muller, "Churchill's Understanding of Politics," 295–96. Writing in the 1870s, Walter Bagehot expressed similar worries about how the enfranchisement would erode responsible government (*Physics and Politics, or thoughts on the application of principles of natural selection and inheritance to political society*). I thank Tom Bateman for this reference.

31 Emmert, *Winston S. Churchill on Empire*, 60.

32 See R. M. Douglas' description of the Allied expulsion of 12 to 14 million German-speaking civilians living in eastern Europe (*Orderly and Humane: The Expulsion of the Germans After the Second World War*, 1–5, 85–92). On Churchill's support during the Russian Revolution of the Balts, whom his cabinet colleague H. A. L. Fisher described as "the proudest and hardest aristocracy in Europe," see Clifford Kinvig, *Churchill's Crusade: The British Invasion of Russia, 1918–1920*, especially Chapter 8.

benevolent and good for the conquered.[33] The great danger of empire then is that in aiming to glorify the excellence of one's own parliamentary regime, one ends up becoming its opposite. Imperial rule, then, may not be a "natural" extension of parliamentary democracy.

Despite Churchill's devotion to parliamentary democracy, his focus on national greatness led him to neglect advocating what might seem to be the real greatness of parliamentary democracy. As we saw above, his focus on leading the war effort led him to neglect domestic British politics, and his failure to manage the debates surrounding the Beveridge Report led to the debacle of him losing the 1945 election.[34] Indeed, domestic affairs bored him.[35] Perhaps he was blind to this possibility of greatness, or perhaps, he did see it but thought it was not an option because of the decadence of parliamentary democracy in the 1930s. Even so, the great danger of imperial rule is that one becomes a lonely, cynical, and blood-soaked provincial administrator in the middle of nowhere. Political ambition conducted through imperial rule can end up with a supremely apolitical result, like Aristotle's god-like or beast-like man who "is incapable of participating or who is in need of nothing through being self-sufficient."[36] Or consider too the reflections of T. E. Lawrence, one of Churchill's friends, who despaired how much he had to sell false promises to his Arab comrades in order to pursue British war and imperial aims. Whether or not empire can benefit rulers and ruled, it contains the real possibility that one must eventually betray one's friends.[37]

The greatness of parliamentary democracy, like Aristotle's polity, is that citizens share in ruling. Ruling may display the measure of the man but Churchill also understood how parliamentary democracy, or party

---

33 I borrow the term, "moral sadism," from Barry Cooper, *Alexander Kennedy Isbister: A Respectable Critic of the Honourable Company*, 49–69, 220–23, 283. As Cooper's study of Isbister shows, "moral sadism" is especially pronounced among imperialists.

34 Schneer, *Ministers at War*, chapters 10–12.

35 Ibid., 261.

36 Aristotle, *Politics*, 1253a28.

37 For reflections on the moral ambiguities of empire, see the essays in David Tabachnick and Toivo Koivukoski, *Enduring Empire: Ancient Lessons for Global Politics*.

government, enables men to display their measure also by being ruled. His service as Leader of the Opposition immediately after leading Great Britain to victory in World War Two is a case in point. He served in this role for six years (July 1945 to October 1951). More than that, though Parliament is supreme, parliamentary democracy allows for multiple jurisdictions, including provinces and states (in federal systems, which Great Britain is not), municipalities, and various organizations in civil society. Parliamentary democracy requires a populace practiced in the arts of self-government, and lower levels of jurisdiction can be seen as junior partners that prepare publicly-minded citizens for work at higher levels. Parliamentary democracy holds out the promise for publicly-spirited individuals that they need not become beasts living outside the walls of the polis, nor die shamefully and, as with General Charles George Gordon, end up decapitated at Khartoum courtesy of the Mahdi. Instead, they can serve as mayor of Dibley or Meryton. Churchill's focus was not on his Oldham constituency but on national affairs. Like most other major thinkers and statesmen in modernity, he regarded the greatness of the national parliament and its place in the nation's system of self-government as the entirety of where self-government takes place. Yet, as Alexis de Tocqueville and Thomas Jefferson understood of the United States, as John George Bourinot knew of Canada, and as much of English history indicates, the city or the township is the locus of self-government and liberty.[38]

Churchill may have judged "mass democracy" too far advanced for a rejuvenation of public life along the lines outlined here. Indeed, his justification of "civilizing empire" as an antidote to the materialism and decadence of mass democracy compares with that of Tocqueville

---

38 Tocqueville, *Democracy in America*, 56–75; on Jefferson, see Hannah Arendt, *On Revolution*, 215–81 (this is part of her discussion and advocacy of "council democracy," where she describes how politics takes place "spontaneously" in power vacuums when national governments have collapsed); on Bourinot, see my "Liberal Education Embedded in Civic Education for Responsible Government: The Case of John George Bourinot," 44–76. *Bourinot's Rules of Order*, a book of parliamentary procedure for business and other types of meetings, was intended as civic education for parliamentary democracy.

himself.[39] However, I have found no evidence of him even contemplating its possibilities. Had Churchill been more consistent in his devotion to parliamentary democracy as political friendship, he would have been more attentive to the "glory" of the "little man," not alone in the voting booth, but attending meetings and being an active citizen exercising self-government. Subsidiarity or sphere sovereignty, where citizens exercise self-rule at various levels of society, seems to be a natural extension of the political friendship that characterizes parliamentary democracy. Indeed, Churchill did see this dimly during the war with his romantic vision of small groups of Britons exercising initiative and improvisation to defend their homeland under conditions of modern warfare: "any kind of local team that mobilized itself for the war effort: Home Guard units, farmers digging tank traps, workers organizing overtime production, Women's Institute ladies making jam, kids collecting scrap metal."[40]

That Churchill saw a form of spontaneous politics among citizens during war—more so than in the form of "council democracy" during times of peace—may in fact be the point. If it is the case, as Churchill claims in his essay, "Shall We All Commit Suicide?," that "[t]he story of the human race is War. Except for brief and precarious interludes there has never been peace in the world; and before history began murderous strife was universal and unending,"[41] then war and empire may take precedence over peace and deliberation as the characteristic political activity by which man's

---

39 In the Introduction to her edition of Tocqueville's writings on empire and slavery, Jennifer Pitts observes: "With weak leaders capable only of petty quibbling, and a divided and apathetic public, France, in Tocqueville's view, required new occasions for virtuous or glorious action. The conquest of Algeria, and in the 1840s the debate over the abolition of slavery in the French Antilles, provided precisely such occasions" ("Introduction," in Tocqueville, *Writings on Empire and Slavery*, xvii). Even so, Tocqueville regarded British imperialism superior to the French version because the British were founding "vibrant, self-governing towns, as well as frontier cities like Cincinnati" (xv). In other words, British "civilizing empire" involved the spread of self-government instead of merely serving the cause of economic exploitation. I thank Daniel J. Mahoney for pointing out the similarities between Churchill and Tocqueville on these points.

40 Rose, *The Literary Churchill*, 335.

41 Churchill, "Shall We All Commit Suicide?," *Thoughts and Adventures*, 259.

measure will be revealed. If that were so, then the emperor who is widely recognized and honoured, not political friendship, would be the essence of political activity, the form of politics as it were.

Conversely, Churchill as statesman also understood that peace is the goal that the art of the warrior serves. His own statesmanship stands as a rebuke to his own exaggerated claim that the human story is war. He was the "judicious person" who ends "universal and unending" strife, as described by Tilo Schabert: "A judicious person does not seek conflict for the sake of conflict. No judicious person develops, when feud comes his or her way, a passionate love for conflict and wants it to never end. The judicious person's courage for war is a courage for peace. The conflict of the world founders when it comes up against the judicious person."[42] The "judicious person" sees peace as the purpose of war.

Conclusion

Churchill never reconciled adequately his imperialism with his devotion to parliamentary democracy—especially its benefits for average citizens. This is not to say he was a deficient friend of the Britons or that his imperialism was necessarily hypocritical. As noted above, by the 1930s he seems to have regarded empire as a possible way to rejuvenate the public spirit of Britons because mass democracy had undermined it. He may have thought the Jeffersonian and Tocquevillian vision of self-rule as unrealistic or impossible in a time of technology and mass democracy.

Churchill was a great friend of the Britons not only because he led them in their darkest hour. He was their great friend for reasons that are consistent with the Jeffersonian and Tocquevillian vision of self-rule. More than sending Britons to rule themselves at various subnational levels, he strove to teach them the arts of self-rule through his writings, most notably in *The Second World War*, but also in *The World Crisis* and in *Marlborough*. He taught them self-rule from his top-level view because it is there that the greatest demands on one's virtue are placed. Ruling does indeed reveal the man, not when he is emperor, but when he is teacher of his people.

42   Tilo Schabert, "A Continuing Strife Towards Cosmogony: History."

The pedagogical nature of his writings can be seen in the way he places the reader in the first-person perspective of the action. He narrates his story by referring the reader to memos written at the time because those reveal the knowledge Churchill had at the time he made his decisions. As narrator, he only reflects upon or judges those actions in retrospect after the reader has had a chance to see the view from the driver's seat, as it were.[43]

The reader of Churchill's memoirs (and the *Marlborough* biography, as discussed in the following chapters) is in the same position as an Athenian who receives a civic education by attending the performance of a tragedy. In his *Poetics*, Aristotle describes how tragedy is a form of civic education because it places spectators within the perspective of the main character. As theorists in the original meaning of the term, spectators identify with the character and think through the plot with the character.[44] Their self-identification with the main character produces a degree of sympathy, while their distance as spectators from the main character enables a degree of reflective distance.

As civic teacher to his readers, Churchill writes with this double perspective in his main works. In the next two chapters, I consider his masterpiece of political wisdom and his most friendly work, his biography of Marlborough.

43 I owe this insight to James Muller, "A Lesson That Had Sunk into His Nature: The Dangers of a Subordinate Position." Muller's paper focuses on Churchill's *The World Crisis* but the pedagogical strategy is found in his other memoirs and historical works.

44 See my *The Form of Politics: Aristotle and Plato on Friendship*, Chapter 3.

Part Four
Friendship and the "Sum of Things"

Chapter Eight
Marlborough's Daimonic Friendliness

It was a means of expressing a vision of men and events seen through what Deakin called "the prism of a superb historical imagination." Thus history was not a "subject," like geography or physics; rather, it was to WSC "the sum of things."[1]

One rule of conduct alone survives as a guide to men in their wanderings: fidelity to covenants, the honour of soldiers, and the hatred of causing human woe.[2]

Marlborough *as the "Sum of Things"*

Churchill wrote his biography of his great ancestor, John Churchill, Duke of Marlborough, ostensibly to counter the claims of Thomas Babington Macaulay and other historians about Marlborough's apparent failures as military commander, the sheer luck of his victories, his reliance upon Prince Eugene's professional knowledge for his victories, corruption, and selfishness, all of which culminated in "Macaulay's story of the betrayal of the expedition against Brest": that was "an obstacle I could not face."[3] Churchill attempts to repudiate their charges and

1   David Dilks, *Churchill and Company*, 33, quoting F. W. Deakin, *Churchill the Historian*, 1.
2   Churchill, *Marlborough*, vol. 2, 996.
3   Churchill, *Marlborough*, vol. 1, 18. For background, see Roy Jenkins, *Churchill: A Biography*, 447–63. For the manner in which Macaulay's *History of England* serves as the "foundation for his own study" of English history in general, see James Muller, "'A Good Englishman': Politics and War in Churchill's Life of Marlborough," 89.

presents Marlborough as the greatest military and political leader Great Britain has ever known.

More than his attempt to save Marlborough's reputation, however, what strikes the reader with this biography, published first in 1933 with subsequent volumes appearing up until 1938 (the time of the Munich Agreement), are the parallels Churchill draws with his contemporary situation. Indeed, like much of his other writings on great figures, Churchill is a self-narrator while he expounds on the political wisdom of others. That he strove to imitate his great ancestor can be seen in the fact that he attributed the same text of Deuteronomy to himself as he did to Marlborough: "Though shalt not muzzle the ox when he is trampling out the corn."[4] This work serves the author's own education in statesmanship during what he would later call the "gathering storm." It is, in James Muller's words, the "capstone of his own political education."[5] It is an example of moral history, the same genre Churchill provides with more explicit tones in his *Second World War*.[6] Of course Churchill's education in statesmanship took place over the course of his entire life, and his earlier works, especially *The World Crisis*, testify to his understanding of statesmanship.

Yet, *Marlborough* was written during the important "exile years" and led his wife, Clementine, to claim that writing it had taught him patience: "It would have surprised them to learn that

4   Deuteronomy 25:4. Churchill, *Marlborough*, vol. 2, 806. Churchill responded with this line when Charles Masterman piously admonished him for being too ambitious (Paul Addison, "Destiny, History, and Providence: The Religion of Winston Churchill" 243).

5   James Muller, "'A Good Englishman': Politics and War in Churchill's Life of Marlborough," 86. Leo Strauss's assessment, in his eulogy of Churchill, of the work bears mentioning: "His Marlborough—the greatest historical work written in our century, is an inexhaustible mine of political wisdom and understanding, which should be required reading for every student of political science" ("Churchill's Greatness"). See also Morton Frisch, "The Intention of Churchill's 'Marlborough,'" 560–74.

6   In his editor's introduction, John Keegan explains that Churchill "would have despised the label of a scientific historian. Like Clarendon and Macaulay, he saw history as a branch of moral philosophy. Indeed, he gave his history a Moral" (Churchill, *The Second World War*, vol. 1, x).

Churchill was far more patient than of old. Nonetheless, Mrs. Churchill told the Prime Minister of Canada that it was indeed so. She explained how the writing of *Marlborough* had produced a real effect upon her husband's character; he had discovered that Marlborough's patience became the secret of his achievements."[7] His good friend Beaverbrook claimed that in World War Two Churchill was more patient, "good tempered and had good feeling for his fellow men" than in previous years.[8] Further, Jenkins suggests the "writing of *Marlborough*, as well as his tastes and thought patterns, made continental Europe, and above all France, Britain's supplement as the centre of the world for him."[9] Writing *Marlborough* reoriented him in important ways.

Many of the lessons he learns from Marlborough are ones he would implement during his own fight against Hitler. As Manfred Weidhorn observes, "By a curious historical irony, Churchill reached the climax of his narrative at the same time that the swirl of current events rose to a whirlwind pitch . . . . Instead of a historical reconstruction, the *Marlborough* had become an exemplary tale with a depressingly familiar pattern."[10] The main threat to British liberty and security is a despot in the middle of the continent; Marlborough must lead an alliance of continental nations against that despot and encircle him on several fronts; naval control of the Mediterranean is necessary, even before engaging the enemy on the continent (an instance of requiring patience); the necessity of a vast network of personal spies; Marlborough's failure to possess both military command and leadership of the House of Commons, which Churchill would make a point of combining when he became Prime Minister; the threat a great war leader poses to the established political order; the tragic fall of a great war leader at the hands of those at home which Churchill too would suffer, though by less severe and less humiliating

7   Dilks, *Churchill and Company*, 58.
8   Young, *Churchill and Beaverbrook*, 141.
9   Jenkins, *Churchill: A Biography*, 600.
10 Manfred Weidhorn, *A Harmony of Interests: Explorations in the Mind of Sir Winston Churchill*, 79–80. Chapter Four of Weidhorn's book extensively compares the two Churchills, especially as those comparisons existed in Churchill's own mind.

means, by losing the election in 1945;[11] the necessity of keeping friendships and covenants with allies as a way of preserving not only national honour but also national security and prosperity; and perhaps most important of all, friendship with one's greatest ally with whom to share a Clausewitzian *coup d'oeil* of the whole scene and to inspire member armies to fight "as if they were the army of a single nation."[12]

As Marlborough had his Eugene of Savoy, so too Churchill would need his Roosevelt. But as Queen Anne and her circle humiliated Marlborough at the summit of his achievements, Churchill, as we saw in the previous chapters, instead viewed himself the servant of Parliament, and friend of parliamentarians: he would ensure he led.[13] His biography, which enabled him to look back so he could look forward, then can be understood as his statement of the "sum of things," his account of the nature of politics and statesmanship. At the center of his account of the nature of politics and statesmanship is friendship.

The capacity to form friendships, not just alliances or strategic partnerships, is, with magnanimity, the central criterion Churchill brings for judging Marlborough and those he associated with. He understood friendship roughly the same way that Aristotle described virtue-friendship, and that is the standard he uses to judge the success or failure of the historic figures he examines in the biography. For instance, King William was competent and had a good strategic mind, but he lacked Marlborough's ability to develop a network of friends to achieve strategic objectives:

> These incomplete relationships were the King's own fault,
> and a misfortune to his reign. If in 1689 and 1690 William,

11 He describes the purpose of the biography's final volume: "It shows how when victory has been won across measureless hazards it can be cast away by the pride of a victorious War Party and the intrigues of a pacifist reaction" (*Marlborough*, vol. 2, 491). See also vol. 2, 783.

12 Churchill, *Marlborough*, vol. 2, 601.

13 The final volume of Churchill's *The Second World War* ends with his concession speech after the 1945 election, with the last word of that speech, and the six-volume work, being "servant" (Churchill, *The Second World War*, vol. 6, 484).

with two kingdoms to govern and the diplomacy of half of Europe in his hands, he treated Marlborough fairly and had not denied him his rightful opportunity upon the battlefields, he might have found that talisman of victory without which all his painstaking, adroit combinations and noble exertions could but achieve a mediocre result. He might have found across the differences of rank that same comradeship, never disturbed by doubt or jealousy, true to the supreme tests of war and fortune, which later shone between Marlborough and Eugene.[14]

Churchill notes that Marlborough had "close friendly relations" with figures including the future Queen Anne, Lord Godolphin (the later Treasurer), and Robert Harley, the Speaker of the House of Commons whose friendship Marlborough could use to influence that institution. Marlborough's so-called "Cockpit" friendships (named after the home of then-Princess Anne) with his wife, Sarah, Princess Anne (later Queen), and Lord Godolphin were pivotal: "The Cockpit friendships were the crucible from which the power and glory of England were soon to rise gleaming among nations."[15]

Marlborough regarded friendship as an important tool for statecraft. He cultivated a network of friends who could help him achieve his political and strategic goals. It was not enough that they be casual acquaintances or friendships of utility. They had truly to be virtue-friends upon whom Marlborough could count. Eugene and Godolphin stand out. Marlborough's other friends were either in the end unreliable (Harley) or outright betrayed him (Queen Anne).

But friendship is not simply a useful tool for statecraft. It is also an end in itself whose purpose transcends politics. This can be seen in two ways. The first is that Churchill credits Marlborough as military commander for giving birth to a national consciousness for Great Britain that

14 Churchill, *Marlborough*, vol. 1, 441. For details on Marlborough's friendship with Heinsius of the Netherlands and others, see *Marlborough*, vol. 1, 520.
15 Churchill, *Marlborough*, vol. 1, 349.

was a precursor to the nationalism that would form the social glue when a more egalitarian England would adopt parliamentary democracy. The second is that his close friendships with Eugene and Godolphin were also an ends in themselves. Marlborough genuinely enjoyed sharing his life of action with those men, especially Eugene. They performed great deeds together and they enjoyed spending time together, probably telling stories to one another and to those present. They took in each other's stories and regarded story-telling as the integral part of politics and friendship, as when Odysseus tells King Alcinous that "the crown of life" involves banqueting and listening to the bard sing.[16] Yet Churchill indicates Marlborough and Eugene were inadequate singers because they thought their actions would speak for them. But Churchill knew better. By writing the biography of Marlborough, Churchill is their bard. As explained in the next chapter, he tells their story and in doing so completes their statesmanship while learning from them. In learning to listen to Marlborough, Churchill would be able to surpass the achievements of his great ancestor.

"The Daemon in Man"

Marlborough marched the British Army, the "red caterpillar," down-country to the Danube to escape the "obstinate" Dutch meddling in his command and to meet up with Eugene. There they each found salvation in one another as friends and allies:

> Both, moreover, possessed the highest outlook on the war; for Eugene, though in the field, was still head of the Imperial War Council, and Marlborough was not only Commander-in-Chief of the English and Dutch armies, but very largely a Prime Minister as well. They could therefore feel toward the whole problem a responsibility different from that of the leaders of individual armies, however large . . . . Each felt the relief which comes from the shadows of a great rock in a thirsty land. In the midst of the intrigues, cross-purposes, and

16 Homer, *Odyssey*, IX.1–12. See discussion in Chapter One, above.

half-measures of a vast, unwieldy coalition trying to make war, here was the spirit of concord, design, and action.[17]

Churchill alludes to Isaiah 32:2 to compare the delight and solace the two men had in joining to the relief of a "great rock in a thirsty land." The alliance against King Louis XIV required a deep sense of like-mindedness and friendship between Marlborough and Eugene, whose friendship undoubtedly was based in part by their both possessing the "highest outlook on the war" for each country. As presidents of the United States claim of their friendships with past presidents, only those past presidents have any idea of the moral, political, and spiritual demands that such power and responsibility of office place on an individual.[18]

Moreover, both possessed a *coup d'oeil* that Carl von Clausewitz, in *On War*, indicates enable great rulers and military leaders to discern the motions and patterns of battle that only military genius can discern:

> Nothing but genius, the daemon in man, can answer the riddles of war, and genius, though it may be armed, cannot be acquired, either by reading or experience. In default of genius nations have to make war as best they can, and since that quality is much rarer than the largest and purest diamonds, most wars are mainly tales of muddle. But when from time to time it flashes upon the scene, order and design with a sense almost of infallibility draw out from hazard and confusion. "The mere aspirant after a type of character only shows his hopeless inferiority when the natural orator or fighter or lover comes along."[19]

Each shared the paramount position of commanding his army in harmony with the other. His reference to William James's discussion of the "daemon

---

17 Churchill, *Marlborough*, vol. 1, 774.
18 Nancy Gibbs and Michael Duffy, *The Presidents Club: Inside the World's Most Exclusive Fraternity.*
19 Churchill, *Marlborough*, vol. 1, 569–70, citing William James, *The Varieties of Religious Experience*, Lectures XI, XII, and XIII, "Saintliness."

in man" is essentially Platonic and fits with his comment about the "burning bush" within Moses (as discussed in Chapter Two).

Churchill's description of Marlborough as daimonic is neither fanciful nor idealistic. It is consistent with the description of the intellectual qualities a commander-statesman must have, according to that great realist, Carl von Clausewitz:

> Finally, and without wishing to risk a closer definition of the higher reaches of the spirit, let us assert that the human mind (in the normal meaning of the term) is far from uniform. If we then ask what sort of mind is likeliest to display the qualities of military genius, experience and observation will both tell us that it is the inquiring rather than the creative mind, the comprehensive rather than the specialized approach, the calm rather than the excitable head to which in war we would choose to entrust the fate of our brothers and children, and the safety and honour of our country.[20]

Clausewitz's account of the commander is comparable indeed to Plato's philosopher or his "spiritual man" (*daimonos aner*). Both are "inquiring" minds and seek "comprehensive" knowledge of their situations. Clausewitz's reticence of wishing to avoid risking "a closer definition of the higher reaches of the spirit" suggests something intangible or daimonic about that demiurgic power of wresting order out of chaos.

Churchill in his writings, including *The Second World War*, frequently speaks of the importance of viewing the "whole scene" of the theater of battle.[21] Meeting other world leaders, in friendship, was paramount in grasping it.[22] In "A Second Choice," he speaks of surveying "the scene of my past life as a whole" to conclude he would not wish to live it all again.[23] Some like Neville Chamberlain thought for Churchill

20 Carl von Clausewitz, *On War*, 112. On the Platonic elements of Clausewitz, see Barry Cooper, "Aron's Clausewitz," 75–104.
21 Churchill, *The Second World War*, vol. 1, 601. General George Marshall could also grasp the "whole scene" (ibid., vol. 4, 726).
22 Churchill, *The Second World War*, vol. 5, 358.
23 Churchill, "A Second Choice," in *Thoughts and Adventures*, 13.

this synoptic vision led to overly simplistic judgments and plans that overlooked details: "In consideration of affairs his decisions are never founded on exact knowledge, nor on careful prolonged considerations of pros and cons. He seeks instinctively for the large and preferably the novel idea such is capable of representation by the broadest brush."[24]

But Churchill recognized the importance of attending to details, or fine brushes, as when he provides his own account of this *coup d'oeil*, comparing the intellectual activity of painting with commanding:

> Trying to paint a picture is, I suppose, like trying to fight a battle. It is, if anything, more exciting than fighting it successfully. But the principle is the same. It is the same kind of problem, as unfolding a long, sustained, interlocked argument. It is a proposition which, whether of few or numberless parts, is commanded by a single unity of conception. And we think—though I cannot tell—that painting a great picture must require an intellect on the grand scale. There must be that all-embracing view which presents the beginning and the end, the whole and each part, as one instantaneous impression retentively and untiringly held in the mind. When we look at the larger Turners—canvases yards wide and tall—and observe that they are all done in one piece and represent one single second of time, and that every innumerable detail, however small, however distant, however subordinate, is set forth naturally and in its true proportion and relation, without effort, without failure, we must feel in presence of an intellectual manifestation the equal in quality and intensity of the finest achievements of warlike action, of forensic argument, or of scientific or philosophical adjudication.[25]

24 Jenkins, *Churchill: A Biography*, 416, citing Randolph Churchill and Martin Gilbert, *Companion Volumes [The Churchill War Papers]*, V, part I, pp. 1328–29.

25 Churchill, "Painting as a Pastime," *Thoughts and Adventures*, 237–38. For discussion about the ramifications of the idea expressed in this essay for Churchill's statesmanship, see Arnn, *Churchill's Trial*, 60–68 and Eliot A. Cohen, "Churchill at War," 42–43.

This painting method of obtaining the "whole scene" compares with his stated historiographic method of explaining Marlborough's life: "In a portrait or impression the human figure is best shown by its true relation to the objects and scenes against which it is thrown, and by which it is defined."[26] *Coup d'oeil*, then, is not restricted to the military commander. It is the same faculty used by the painter, historian, and philosopher: each aspires for the synoptic vision that takes in every detail and every proportion.

Churchill emphasizes these very daimonic and demiurgic qualities in Marlborough:

> He possessed a combination of mental, moral, and physical qualities adapted to action which were so lifted above the common run as to seem almost godlike. His appearance, his serenity, his piercing eye, his gestures, the tones of his voice—nay the beat of his heart—diffused a harmony upon all around him. Every word he spoke was decisive. Victory often depended upon whether he rode half a mile this way or that.[27]

His gift for friendship also gave him extraordinary powers to place himself in the shoes of his enemy, so that he could usually anticipate his moves: "He forecasted with perfect comprehension the future action of the enemy. His power of putting himself in the enemy's shoes, and measuring truly what they ought to do, and what he himself would most dislike, was one of his greatest gifts. He was only wrong in his anticipations when the enemy made a mistake."[28] Marlborough's "measurements of men and affairs were so sure that he seems almost gifted with prophetic power."[29] He possessed an "occult common sense" with the power of divination.[30] Churchill cites the judgment of historian Onno Klopp who

---

26 Churchill, *Marlborough*, vol. 1, 19.
27 Ibid., 571.
28 Churchill, *Marlborough*, vol. 2, 430.
29 Ibid., 275.
30 Churchill, *Marlborough*, vol. 1, 761.

compared his sense to "the words of a soothsayer."[31] Accordingly, he refers to unspecified "modern research" (probably Klopp) for showing "how truly Marlborough divined or measured facts."[32]

Part of Marlborough's daimonic power of divining facts includes his capacity to divine the characters of those around him. His assessment of Queen Anne is a case in point: "His eye, which measured things so exactly and pierced into the thoughts and motives of men and women, had told him the truth about the Queen."[33] Similarly, Churchill cites Voltaire's description of Marlborough, "who, by a long course of experience, had learned the art of diving into the real characters of men, and discovering the connexion between their most secret thoughts and their actions, gestures, and discourse."[34] This he did by watching their actions and knowing their interests, but also in conversation and in their casual remarks, frequently at dinner parties: "Often in the casual remarks of great men one learns their true mind in an intimate way."[35] Indeed, Churchill points out that, "Marlborough did not belong to the stern and silent type of men of action. On the contrary, he was affable and talkative. People learned from his easy and genial flow of conversation what he wanted them to know."[36]

Of course his daimonic powers could not always ensure success. For example he knew Queen Anne would betray him but there was nothing he could do about it. Yet, Churchill claims these powers ensured his success so far as he could go: "Perhaps this extraordinary quality of using audacity and circumspection as if they were tools to be picked up or laid down according to the job is the explanation of his never being entrapped in ten years of war. His mind was a weighing machine for practical affairs as perfect as has ever been known."[37] In essence, Marlborough's

31   Churchill, *Marlborough*, vol. 2, 225. Klopp, *Der Fall des Hauses Stuart*, vol. xii, 387.
32   Churchill, *Marlborough*, vol. 2, 71.
33   Ibid., 409.
34   Ibid., 226, citing *Histoire de Charles XII*, 225.
35   Ibid., 225. See also ibid., 70. See Chapter One of this study for Churchill's own use of dinners in his statecraft.
36   Churchill, *Marlborough*, vol. 1, 732.
37   Ibid., 955.

daimonic powers were an example of the capacity to know soul and souls, which Aristotle claims is essential for a good ruler: "It is clear that one who is skilled in politics needs to know in some way the things that concern the soul, just as one who is going to cure the eyes must also know about the whole body. So the one skilled in politics must study the soul, but must study it for the sake of political concerns."[38] It is insufficient for the ruler to possess textbook knowledge of the parts of the soul, which Aristotle (following Plato) enumerates. Rather, the good ruler must also understand individual souls, which is learned in part by understanding the actions performed by those individuals. The practice of friendship enables one to see more deeply into souls of friends, acquaintances, and even enemies because the very point of the practice is to come into "intimate acquaintance" with the ethos of another.[39]

Marlborough's daimonic powers, which seemed to facilitate his capacity for friendship, made him an exemplary commander and statesman: "It is these qualities of *perfect comprehensive judgment*, serene in disappointment or stress, unbiased by the local event in which he was himself involved, this fixing with untiring eye and *absolute selflessness* the problem as a whole, that deserve the study and respect of soldiers of every age."[40] Churchill sees an essential link between "perfect comprehensive judgment" and "absolute selflessness." The capacity to be politically prudent depends upon the capacity to practice virtue-friendship, with the latter capacity also depending upon the former. They inform one another. His observation of Marlborough here compares with Churchill's observation,

---

38 Aristotle, *Nicomachean Ethics*, 1102a20–25. Aristotle in this same passage seems to suggest the statesman need not concern himself with the soul beyond political concerns, which suggests they need not contemplate more philosophical questions such as those he treats in his *On the Soul*. Even so, his comparison of knowing soul to eye doctors also needing to know "the whole body" suggests the statesman does require knowledge of soul that somehow goes beyond soul. My focus in this discussion of Churchill's description of Marlborough's daimonic powers attempts to follow that track. In this discussion Churchill is more Platonic than Aristotelian, because Plato certainly views this kind of power as part of the statesman's capacity.
39 See Aristotle, *Nicomachean Ethics*, 1158a16.
40 Churchill, *Marlborough*, vol. 2, 373. Emphasis added.

in his essay on Asquith discussed in Chapter One, that political prudence has an essential connection with the capacity for conversation.

Churchill's assessment of Marlborough should not be viewed as an exaggeration, at least not as a general description of human capacity. As his description of the "genius, the daemon in man" shows, political and military greatness involves an indescribable "extra" on top of all the other tangible qualities of leadership and intelligence. It involves the capacity to take in the "whole scene." Of course daimonism cannot be measured or "proven." It seems one can only recognize it in another when one possesses it, and Churchill seemed to possess it.

Friends with the "Highest Outlook"

The friendship of Marlborough and Eugene began in the letters they shared with one another in 1701–02, which led them to meet and cement their friendship in a banquet on June 10, 1704:

> Then at once began that glorious brotherhood in arms which neither victory nor misfortune could disturb, before which jealousy and misunderstanding were powerless, and of which the history of war furnishes no equal example. The two men took to one another from the outset. They both thought and spoke about war in the same way, measured the vast forces at work by the same standards, and above all alike looked to a great battle with its awful risks as the means by which their problems would be solved.[41]

They were friends and they displayed their friendship:

> Once Eugene had joined Marlborough their perfect comradeship and pre-eminence established a higher unity of command than had ever been seen in the war. "The Princes,"

---

41 Churchill, *Marlborough*, vol. 1, 774. Churchill compares the "comradeship" of Generals Robert Lee and Stonewall Jackson to that of Marlborough and Eugene (vol. 2, 86, and *History of the English Speaking Peoples*, vol. 4, 171).

as they came to be called in the confederacy, settled everything between themselves. Neither ever allowed a whisper of disagreement to circulate. They were apparently immune from any kind of jealousy of each other, were proof against every form of mischief-making or intrigue, and in the field at any rate were in practice absolute . . . . Without this new fact at the allied headquarters the extraordinary operations which these chapters describe, so intricate, so prolonged, and contrary on many occasions to the accepted principles of war, could never have been achieved.[42]

Elsewhere Churchill claims: "So perfect was the harmony which the ascendancy of Marlborough and Eugene exercised upon all minds that these soldiers of different races, creeds, and Governments—English, Scots, Irish, Danes, Prussians, Hanoverians, Hessians, Saxons, Palatines, and Dutch—acted together as if they were the army of a single nation."[43] Churchill would undoubtedly have held this example in mind during World War Two when he and Roosevelt used their friendship to forge the alliance "as if they were the army of a single nation."

They felt the strains of each other's battles as if they were each man's own, and Eugene offered succor to Marlborough who suffered from depression.[44] Eugene signed some of his letters to Marlborough, "Your affectionate Cousin" and Marlborough claimed, "I not only esteem, but really love that Prince."[45] Churchill describes their friendship in terms comparable to Aristotle's language of virtue-friends as one's "second self."

Despite the differences of their backgrounds and personalities, they shared an intellectual vision not only of the necessary means of defeating their common enemy, but also a moral and intellectual vision of human excellence:

42 Churchill, *Marlborough*, vol. 2, 331.
43 Ibid., 601.
44 Ibid., 350, 370.
45 Ibid., 182, 220, 251.

Marlborough, the model husband and father, concerned with building up a home, founding a family, and gathering a fortune to sustain it: Eugene, a bachelor—nay, almost a misogynist—disdainful of money, content with his bright sword and his lifelong animosities against Louis XIV. Certainly quite different kinds of men; yet when their eyes met each recognized a kindred spirit in all that governs war. They were in action, as has been well said, "two bodies with one soul."[46]

Churchill's comment here must be in conjunction with the quotation above regarding the "daemon in man," that Clausewitzian *coup d'oeil* whereby military and political genius is capable of perceiving the whole scene. Prior to making that comment regarding the "daemon in man," Churchill states that the highest solution of viewing the scene "must be evolved from the eye and brain and soul of a single man, which from hour to hour are making subconsciously all the unweighable adjustments, no doubt with many errors, but with an ultimate practical accuracy."[47] Yet later he claims "no one can comprehend the movements leading up to the battle of Blenheim unless he realizes that Eugene and Marlborough were working like two lobes of the same brain. They were in constant touch with one another."[48] And quite often they did not need to be in touch with one another:

Marlborough and Eugene in their battles understood one another so well that each exercised a supervision over the entire field. But although there was no formal division of spheres, Eugene assumed the direction of this great operation upon the right, while Marlborough, with his headquarters staff, conducted the general battle from a slight eminence about

46 Churchill, *Marlborough*, vol. 1, 774–75. Churchill's quotation of "two bodies with one soul" echoes a saying usually attributed to Aristotle, not to any particular attribution anyone else made to Marlborough and Eugene. It does not appear in any of Aristotle's extant writings, but Diogenes attributes the statement to him in his *Lives of the Eminent Philosophers*, V.i.18.
47 Churchill, *Marlborough*, vol. 1, 569.
48 Ibid., 825.

half-way between the Grant Battery and the village of Blareg-
nies.[49]

Churchill claims of Marlborough's victory at Malplaquet: "Marlborough's fame, his influence upon the Continent, his comradeship with
Eugene, had compelled the tremendous event."[50]

Churchill suggests then that the pair enjoyed not just a Clausewitzian
coup d'oeil separately as individuals, but together as friends. His analysis
is comparable to the way that Aristotle describes the peak of friendship
as a joint intellectual perception, in Greek *sunaisthesis*, the joint or mutual perception of the good whereby friends behold one another insepa-
rably as they behold the good.[51] For Churchill, it seems their military
and political success was predicated upon this sunaisthetic *coup d'oeil*.
It was also something he enjoyed with Roosevelt, as we saw in previous
chapters. That shared vision enabled them also to view their friendship
not only as one of shared political and strategic vision, but also the very
purpose of that statecraft. Their friendship seemed to be based upon
something higher than mere politics or strategy.

They had fun together. They were at play together. As warriors they
sought the "decisive battle" that not only would defeat Louis XIV once
and for all, but they also saw it as the primary means of testing their met-
tle as warriors, indeed their virtue, their very moral ethos. Churchill explains the importance of the Battle of Blenheim: "With pride and
pleasure they rejoiced in each other's companionship and in their conviction that the whole war must be put to the test at dawn."[52] Describing
the importance for them personally of the Battle of Malplaquet,
Churchill explains their play:

> Marlborough, and still more Eugene, had behind him a vast
> experience of war. If they had a plan it was to be no rule. The

---

49 Churchill, *Marlborough*, vol. 2, 605–06, on the battle of Malplaquet.
50 Ibid., 646.
51 See my *The Form of Politics: Aristotle and Plato on Friendship*, Chapter
    2.
52 Churchill, *Marlborough*, vol. 1, 843.

measureless chances of action would certainly create better or worse situations in which they felt competent to deal. Whatever they may have said or written, both looked out upon the day with zest and thrill, and casting care aside, rejoiced in the intensity of risk, will, art, and action which lay before them. Moreover, here must be the end of the long war, and rest and glory after toil. All should be staked. Nothing could be neglected, and nothing should be withheld.[53]

In this remarkable passage, Churchill describes the pair together stripped naked of artifice or plan, and devoid of assistance except of each other. All they knew and were would reach their climax at this battle; none of what they knew or were mattered anymore. Together they would throw themselves directly into the arms of *Fortuna* full of confidence in their own excellence and in each other. They would stake all together and for one another: "nothing should be withheld." Life offers them no better opportunity to shine and they shine together.

Despite Churchill's emphasis on their equality, he does admit that Marlborough was the superior because he was the grand commander of the allied forces against Louis XIV.[54] Churchill observes of Marlborough's Machiavellian streak that: "As clever at piercing the hidden designs of his enemy as in beating him on the field of battle, he united the cunning of the fox to the force of the lion."[55] Later he claims, "He acted thus in the interests of right strategy and of the common cause as he conceived them. He was accustomed by the conditions under which he fought to be continually deceiving friends for their goods and foes for their bane."[56]

Churchill does not explicitly specify the way Marlborough deceived Eugene for his good, but the problems that arose over Marlborough's

---

53 Churchill, *Marlborough*, vol. 2, 603. On Marlborough's thirst for the "decisive battle" and for "venturing all" where his character would face the ultimate test, see also ibid., vol. 2, 437 and 665. On war as play, see Johannes Huizenga, *Homo Ludens*, Chapter 5.

54 Churchill, *Marlborough*, vol. 2, 338, 470.

55 Churchill, *Marlborough*, vol. 1, 761.

56 Churchill, *Marlborough*, vol. 2, 303.

wish to put Toulon to siege would be one example. However, Churchill observes that in the case of the siege of Toulon, which Eugene had opposed and who had suffered so much in waging, Marlborough regretted forcing Eugene to go along with his plan because of the cost it had on their friendship as well as on the war effort: "But the cost was measureless. A year's campaign must be used; a year of political attrition at home; a year of waning comradeship through the Alliance. High stakes for Toulon!"[57] Marlborough regretted the manner in which his disagreement with Eugene harmed their friendship and their capacity to pursue strategic objectives:

> Marlborough's admiration for Eugene, his respect for his vast experience and mastery of the art of war, made it impossible for him to force Eugene beyond his will. In the previous year he had tried to press him unduly about Toulon. It had not succeeded. Indeed, when Eugene differed from him he may well have questioned his own instinct.[58]

Churchill illuminates how their friendship constrained whatever benefits a more Machiavellian approach to politics might have brought for Marlborough. In Churchill's reading, Marlborough was not a Machiavellian prince but was instead a classical prince who, though capable of ruthlessness, has a much clearer sense of the way politics is conducted because it is predicated upon personal relations and friendships.[59]

After Marlborough was removed from office, Eugene paid a visit to him in London in early 1712 as a gesture of loyalty and support for his friend. It was a tense time. There were rumors the two would wage a coup d'état.[60] Eugene made the rounds, meeting various politicians and

---

57   Ibid., 259.
58   Ibid., 401.
59   On the meaning of "classical prince," see Schabert, "A Classical Prince: The Style of François Mitterrand." On the classical prince and friendship, see my "Friendship as Precondition and Consequence of Creativity in Politics."
60   Churchill, *Marlborough*, vol. 2, 924–25. Churchill calls these rumours "rubbish."

important people. Churchill provides little detail on their own time together, highlighting instead Eugene's public demonstrations of his friendship with Marlborough during this time when Marlborough was suffering political attacks from all directions: "Thus did the famous Prince and warrior proclaim his friendship for his comrade of so many glorious days."[61]

The Cockpit Friendships

Churchill's practice of friendship on the "domestic" front of Great Britain focuses on the "Cockpit friendships" that revolved upon Anne, who became Queen when she succeeded her brother-in-law William of Orange. She was also the Protestant daughter to James II, whom Marlborough was instrumental in having deposed. Churchill's biography of Marlborough revolves around the rise and decline of the "Cockpit friendships." These include his wife Sarah, who was for a long time her close friend and one of Anne's ladies of the bedchamber, but whose persistent Whiggism grated on Anne, leading to the dissolution of their friendship.[62]

Sidney Godolphin, as First Lord of the Treasury, was also part of this group. Churchill explains "their unbroken association runs through this story."[63] Marlborough's close friendship with Godolphin ensured a steady flow of funds for Marlborough's military budgets:

> His pole star was Marlborough and Marlborough's war. He saw his supreme duty in forming a Parliamentary foundation upon which Marlborough could bestride Europe, and in furnishing him with supplies of money, men, and ships. To this purpose he used all the ruse and artifice with which forty years of Parliamentary and Court intrigue . . . had made him familiar. While Harley calculated upon the collapse of the party

---

61 Ibid., 926.
62 Ibid., 33.
63 Churchill, *Marlborough*, vol. 1, 51. Churchill refers to him as his faithful friend on several occasions (see vol. 1, 534, vol. 2, 729).

system, Godolphin relied upon its feuds. The Lord Treasurer's strength consisted . . . in his supreme gift for applying the maxim "Divide and govern." His skill lay in the management of business in such a way that, immediately any party assault on the Ministry threatened to become dangerous, some question would be raised to set the Tories and Whigs by the ears. Therefore he worked for national government through equipoise and cancellation of the parties, whereas Harley sought it by the fusion of their central elements.[64]

More than their political alliance, Churchill treats their friendship as one of the few constants woven through both men's tumultuous political careers. Their friendship, as with all the "Cockpit friendships," formed the crucible of the English nation. Its existence is woven through the biography and cannot be summarized without also summarizing the contents of the entire biography. Churchill speaks less about its meaning than he does of Marlborough and Eugene, but his relatively few reflective explanations emphasize the undying loyalty they held for one another. Indeed, as Frances Harris demonstrates, their friendship, which included Sarah Churchill, was indeed a virtue-friendship that was the "actual embodiment" of "the fiscal military state on which Britain's global empire was built in succeeding generations."[65] She adds: "I think it is in this light, rather than in the more commonplace senses of ad hoc political association, patronage, or kinship that we should see the Marlborough-Godolphin friendship."[66]

Churchill describes a particularly difficult time for Godolphin in the autumn of 1706 when the Act of Union was being finalized. He had lost most of his support from Whigs and Tories, and "found himself in daily

---

64 Churchill, *Marlborough*, vol. 2, 295.

65 Frances Harris, *The General in Winter: The Marlborough-Godolphin Friendship and the Reign of Queen Anne*, 1. This book came to my attention very late during the preparation of my book manuscript, and so I have been unable to make full use of its fine and detailed study. It provides an important explanation of the friendship ideal that animated Marlborough, and thus implicitly Winston Churchill.

66 Harris, *The General in Winter*, 3.

contact with a highly discontented Queen" because of her anger at Godolphin and Marlborough for having "pressed upon her" the Act, which required her to accept the succession of the House of Hanover:

> We can see how extremely hazardous was the Lord Treasurer's position. A false step in his personal relations with the Queen on his part, an emotional crisis on hers, and he would see himself delivered to the competitive fury of both bitter factions . . . . Godolphin felt himself in awful jeopardy, and almost without a friend. Almost—but there was one friend, an old friend, the greatest man alive, whom he knew he could count upon till death. He was sure that Marlborough would never desert him; and thus he persevered, and with his perseverance grew the unit of Britain and her power among nations.[67]

Churchill emphasizes the solace they took in one another during their long and bitter battles with their political enemies:

> There is so much bewailing in the Marlborough-Godolphin correspondence, written for no eye but their own, that many writers have questioned the sincerity of these tough, untiring personalities who, in the upshot, held on with extreme tenacity and to the last minute to every scrap of power. It was surely, then, no mere desire to keep up appearances before each other, but rather to fortify their own minds for action by asseverating their own disinterestedness, that made it worthwhile to set all this on paper?[68]

Churchill's assessment of Anne's treatment of Marlborough was seen in a previous chapter. His assessment of her treatment of Godolphin upon dismissing him in August 1710 is no less damning. He praises Godolphin for the high degree of personal integrity as First Lord of the Treasury, which was an unusual characteristic for civil servants at the time: "He quitted his

---

67 Churchill, *Marlborough*, vol. 2, 196.
68 Ibid., 509.

nine years' administration of wartime finance, with all the opportunities of self-enrichment by speculation or by taking presents, apart altogether from direct corruption, without reproach and with barely a thousand pounds a year."[69] Queen Anne promised but broke her promise to provide him with a pension of £4000 per year. By "a curious coincidence" his elder brother died within ten days of his dismissal, which brought him an inheritance of the same amount: "John and Sarah regarded themselves as responsible for his well-being. Their houses were at his disposal. He spent a good deal of the remaining two years of his life at Holywell."[70]

As mentioned above, Churchill claims the "Cockpit friendships were the crucible from which the power and glory of England were soon to rise gleaming among nations."[71] He credits the group, especially Marlborough, with forging the tools necessary for the rise of English power in the world, although this contrasts with his claim in the conclusion of the last volume of the biography that the treachery of Marlborough's enemies also lost the confidence of England's allies and thus caused the immediate decline of its power after the Spanish Wars of Succession.

Churchill also treats this period of history as a key step in England's march toward parliamentary democracy. Events at home and abroad worked in tandem to push history forward. He describes the political and historical significance of the Battle of Blenheim (August 1704): "From across the seas in England the Protestant succession, Parliamentary government, and the future of the British Empire advanced with confident tread. All these had brought their cases before the dread tribunal now set up on this Danube plain."[72] "The charge at Blenheim opened to her the gateways of the modern world."[73] Several key players of the Cockpit helped bring that about, although that was of course not their intention. Men like Godolphin and Marlborough were appointed by the Queen and while they were Tories, they were not party men. While Marlborough's energies were focused upon winning wars, Churchill credits him (and

---

69 Ibid., 744.
70 Ibid.
71 Churchill, *Marlborough*, vol. 1, 349.
72 Ibid., 844.
73 Ibid., 916.

Godolphin as well) with a statesman's understanding of what the common good of England consists, which entails finding a proper balance or, equipoise, to use a favored Burkean term, of the partisan factions. While neither parliamentarians nor party men, both, practicing politics in the wake of the 1688 Act of Settlement, seemed to understand the importance of parties and the role they would have to play in encouraging the "moderating elements" to govern effectively. Though not a member of the Cockpit, Harley as leader of the House of Commons served as the link between them and those factions.

The "Old Corporal" and the English Nation

Churchill also credits Marlborough with promoting a sense of English nationhood and he views the Wars of Succession, and Marlborough in particular, as instrumental in bringing forth a latent sense of political friendship within the combatant nations. The Wars of Spanish Succession invigorated a dormant sense of French and Spanish nationalism:

> In those days, when all the large populations were controlled and their life expressed only by a few thousand notables and educated persons, there was, of course, no conscious movement of the masses. Nevertheless the governing classes throughout France, and also in Spain, derived a strange invigoration from the national spirit. The French people reverenced and almost loved their monarch; and a strong unity reaching far beneath the official hierarchies now made itself felt. A new flood of strength, welling from depths which the early eighteenth century had not plumbed, revived and replenished an enfeebled nobility . . . . They followed also the promptings of the French heart, of which [Louis XIV] had so long been unconscious.[74]

Churchill explains Marlborough's role in helping to bring forth a sense of English nationalism, a form of political friendship, whose

---

74 Churchill, *Marlborough*, vol. 2, 558–59.

primary step was events surrounding the Battle of Blenheim in May 1704. He begins his narrative with the march of the British Army up country—Marlborough's *anabasis*, to use Xenophon's term—to meet up with the forces of Eugene. We saw above how the two friends viewed their meeting as the "relief which comes from the shadows of a great rock in a thirsty land."[75] British nationhood was being forged in the coming-together of the two friends. Churchill explains the significance of the march: "The annals of the British Army contain no more heroic episode than this march from the North Sea to the Danube . . . . The profound calculations which he made, both political and military, could only present a sum of dangers against which forethought could make no provision. All that gallant army that marched with him risked life and honour: but he alone bore the burden. It was for them to obey the lawful authorities. For him the task was to persuade, deceive, and defy them for their own salvation."[76]

Churchill describes Marlborough's ambition as transcending material rewards: "His toils could only be for England, for that kind of law the English called freedom, for the Protestant religion, and always in the background for that figure, half mystic symbol and the rest cherished friend, the Queen."[77] But his ambition transcended even them, taking the form of "the responsibility of proprietorship": "It had become his war. He was the hub of the wheel." The journey upcountry, his *anabasis*, removed him and his army from the distractions and hazards of the politicians and allies. It was just his army and he marching up-country in a journey that forged them together.

Marlborough's troops loved him. He shared their same risks and took care of them: "In the midst of the scene of carnage, with its drifting smoke-clouds, scurrying fugitives, and brightly colored lines, squares, and oblongs of men, he sat on his horse, often in the hottest fire, holding in his mind the position and fortunes of every unit in his army from minute to minute and giving his orders aloud."[78] Churchill contrasts this from current styles of command, "working in calm surroundings, often beyond even the sound of the cannonade." For today's commanders,

75 Churchill, *Marlborough*, vol. 1, 774.
76 Ibid., 740.
77 Ibid., 741.
78 Ibid., 570.

"personal encounters are limited to an unpleasant conversation with an army commander who must be dismissed, an awkward explanation to a harassed Cabinet, or an interview with a representative of the neutral Press . . . . In the process of enlargement the sublime function of military genius—perhaps happily—has been destroyed forever."[79]

In the field he lived simply, unlike most other commanders during this time: "What a pitiful contrast to the style in which the Great Monarch took the field! No mistresses; no actors, no poets, no painters, not even a historian—except the chaplain, Dr. Hare; no proper following of toadies and hangers-on; no roads blocked with convoys of cooks and comforts—just coarse, squalid, simplicity basely interested in saving sixpence!"[80] Marlborough's frugality, or parsimony as his resentful officers viewed it, led his troops to love him because quite frankly it enabled him always to pay them:

> His habit of personal economy extended to the whole control of Marlborough's armies. He was always worrying about the cost of things in a manner that seemed most petty and unbecoming. It was remarkable, indeed, that he was so popular with the troops; but, then, of course he always took care that they got their rations and pay punctually . . . so that the rank and file did not feel his cheese-paring at all, and only saw the victories.[81]

For all these reasons, Marlborough's soldiers loved him and nicknamed him, "the Old Corporal."[82]

Churchill summarizes the solidarity he enjoyed with his troops late in his career, at the Bouchain operation in August-September 1711:

> We find him at sixty-one, in poor health, racked with earache and headache, after ten years of war, making these personal reconnaissances within deadly range of the enemy's entrenchments and batteries in order to make sure that his soldiers were

---

79 Ibid., 571.
80 Ibid., 413.
81 Ibid., 415. See Muller, "'A Good Englishman,'" 88.
82 Churchill, *Marlborough*, vol. 2, 109.

not set impossible tasks and their brave lives not cast needlessly away. Although he was the key of the Grand Alliance, he did not consider his life too precious to be risked. It was because his soldiers felt he was watching over them, and would never spare himself where their welfare and honour were concerned, that they were deeply attached to him. His "attention and care," as Corporal Matthew Bishop wrote, "was over us all." Always patiently and thoroughly examining the conditions on the front of the army, unwearied by the ten campaigns, burdened by no sense of his own importance, undiscouraged by the malice of his enemies at home, he performed to the very end most faithfully and vigilantly the daily duty of a soldier.[83]

One can compare Marlborough's attention to detail and the welfare of his troops to that of Churchill: his solidarity with soldiers in the trenches in World War One after his Gallipoli disgrace, his attention to minor details of ritual for the worship service aboard the H.M.S. *Prince of Wales* in Placentia Bay, or his wish to view the Normandy invasion up front and personal. While both were aristocrats, Churchill imitated Marlborough's common touch that inspired a strong sense of political friendship.

And so Churchill describes the scene of the conquering hero's homecoming after his victory at Blenheim. "In the first days of the new year (January 3 [1704]), all London was to a pageant the like of which England had never seen."[84] Churchill describes Queen Anne's oversight of the pageantry and the long procession of troops with their French prizes through London to Westminster Hall:

> But more significant than this well-organized ceremonial was the temper of the masses who lined the route or thronged behind the procession. The foreign Ambassadors, bred in countries where Court, nobles, and magnates counted for all, were struck by a manifestation of a national self-consciousness unique among the nations. Here was a society which did not

83 Churchill, *Marlborough*, vol. 2, 861.
84 Churchill, *Marlborough*, vol. 1, 915.

end with the powerful and the rich, which descended through every class of citizen down to the very poorest and most humble, all of whose hearts responded to the feeling that it was *their* victory, that *their* cause had triumphed, and that *their* England was growing great. Even while foreign observers caviled with some reason that the London populace claimed for themselves a victory in which their troops had formed but a quarter of the army, they admired the integral force and comprehension of the vigorous islanders, who could quarrel so fiercely with one another and yet rejoice together in national glory.[85]

Churchill describes England of 1704 as a republic in the original sense, a *res publica*, a regime where the common good is not just shared but owned by all factions. Their quarrelsome political friendship astonished the foreign observers who would have expected such quarrelsome behavior to promote strife, just as foreign (and some native) observers today regard the quarrelsomeness of western democracies as a sign of weakness or "civil war by other means." But this "quarreling polity," to borrow Tilo Schabert's phrase, though a paradox, is constituted by political friendship because, as Aristotle points out, one of the things friends do for one another is knocking off each other's rough edges.[86] Friends quarrel because they recognize that they share something worthwhile about which to quarrel. England's quarreling polity was not yet a parliamentary democracy, which we saw in previous chapters is the best form of government according to Churchill, but "the charge at Blenheim opened to her the gateways of the modern world."[87]

Conclusion

Despite Marlborough's many military victories, the tale of *Marlborough* is one of political defeat, not just his at the hands of Queen Anne but

---

85 Churchill, *Marlborough*, vol. 1, 915. Emphasis in original.
86 Schabert, *Boston Politics: The Creativity of Power*, 230; Aristotle, *Nicomachean Ethics*, 1172a17.
87 Churchill, *Marlborough*, vol. 1, 916.

that of England. Churchill judges Anne's betrayal of Marlborough as also a betrayal of England's allies via the Treaty of Utrecht, which did extraordinary harm to England's political fortunes for a generation:

> The mean and treacherous manner in which the Grand Alliance had been broken up, with the shameful episodes of violated faith and desertion in the field, inflicted the stigma which was for so long visible on the face of this transaction. Forty years later William Pitt, writing to Sir Benjamin Keene, feeling the odium which still clung to England and infected her every public pledge, pronounced the stern judgment that "Utrecht was an indelible reproach of the last generation" .... [I]n the century that followed Europe was racked with repeated conflicts and Great Britain fought four separate wars with France, aggregating in all forty-three years of deadly strife. Great coalitions were formed against Britain. She was stripped by war and other causes of her vast American possessions. Her existence as a world state was repeatedly in jeopardy.[88]

Marlborough is a story of the rise and fall of the great man. He fell due to forces beyond his control: the jealousy and envy of the Queen and her circle. They fell, and Great Britain subsequently suffered, because they betrayed their friends. Friendship for Churchill, and keeping faith with one's friends, is closely connected with political success. Churchill indicates as much when he summarizes the moral of the biography: "One rule of conduct alone survives as a guide to men in their wanderings: fidelity to covenants, the honour of soldiers, and the hatred of causing human woe."[89] For Churchill, this was Marlborough's code and helps explain his devotion to his friends.

---

88 Churchill, *Marlborough*, vol. 2, 995. Churchill also attributes Queen Anne's downfall to her failure to keep faith with her friends (*Marlborough*, vol. 2, 1009).
89 Ibid., 996.

Chapter Nine
Churchill's Completion
of Marlborough's Story

It is not often that someone comes along who is a true friend
and a good writer.[1]

Story Telling, Friendship, and the Search for Order

In this chapter, we consider the moral significance of Churchill's biography of Marlborough in order to see the full significance friendship
held for him in the practice of statesmanship. Churchill saw further and
deeper than his great ancestor. For all of Marlborough's skills of statesmanship, his capacity for story-telling, the consummate activity of
friends and of statesmen, was deficient. Story-telling has greater magnitude than idle chatter and even of conversation in which Churchill ex-
celled and saw as a central skill of the statesman. Story-telling has
greater magnitude than these because it is the particular mode by which
political actors explain and judge political action, usually their own. It
might be compared to myth or tragedy, that form of communication that
Aristotle placed midway between history, the narration of facts, and philosophy, the inquiry into the general principles of human purposes.[2]
Story-telling seeks to make sense of actions, and by doing so completes

---

1   E. B. White, *Charlotte's Web*, 184.
2   Aristotle explains: "poetry is a more philosophical and a more serious thing
    than history, since poetry speaks more of things that are universal, and his-
    tory of things that are particular. It is what is universal, the sorts of things
    that in a certain sort of person turns out to say or do as a result of what is
    likely or necessary, that poetry aims at" (Aristotle, *Poetics*, 1451b5–7).

those actions. It is the quintessential form of political friendship, noticed as far back in Homer's *Odyssey*, as discussed in Chapter One. There we saw how Homer has Odysseus, after listening to the bard Demodocus, tell the King of the Phaeacians to whom he is about to narrate his own story (or is Odysseus actually Homer?): "What a fine thing it is to listen to such a bard."[3] Story-telling is the practice of political friendship and constitutes the ethos of Churchill's own sense of political friendship, as seen in his many writings. It was for this reason that, in reviewing a volume of his speeches, Malcolm Cowley exclaimed, "He not only makes laws for his people but writes their songs as well."[4] As a work of moral history, Churchill's *Marlborough* too lies between history understood simply as the narration of facts, and philosophy. Churchill is telling a story, a myth, the essential language of politics, the form of political friendship.

As with many other statesmen, Churchill regarded politics as a battle of ideas because ideas represent the way one aspires to live, and thus to guide action.[5] It is true that nations have interests and statesmen pursue them. However, as Rose asks in his fine study, *The Literary Churchill*, "what are nations interested in?"[6] Rose's answer in relation to Churchill is correct: "Of course they want power, wealth, trade, land, and security. But political actors also act out stories, which can have a force and a momentum of their own, and which may not always serve the more national interests . . . . All politicians, however, tell stories."[7]

Churchill explained this point about stories and ideas early in his career, in *The River War*, when describing the good reasons the Sudanese had in defending themselves against the British Imperialists:

> The desire, which most men and all communities manifest at all times, to associate with their actions at least the appearance of moral right . . . . No community embarks on a great

3   Homer, *Odyssey*, IX.1–12.
4   Malcolm Cowley, "Mr. Churchill Speaks," 537.
5   On Thatcher, see Richard Aldous, *Reagan and Thatcher*, 24.
6   Rose, *The Literary Churchill*, ix.
7   Ibid., ix-x.

enterprise without fortifying itself with the belief that from some points of view its motives are lofty and disinterested .... The sufferings of a people or a class may be intolerable, but before they will take up arms and risk their lives some unselfish and impersonal spirit must animate them.[8]

Political action is impossible without a fortifying moral principle or story that sustains and justifies the deeds performed in the name of that moral principle or story. Churchill suggests that such principles and stories aim to be "unselfish and impersonal" because only then can "most men and all communities" believe themselves in the "moral right." Yet, the difficulty is discerning those that have the "appearance of moral right" from those that truly are morally right. Political action is guided by principles or stories, and such principles and stories themselves stand below the search for truth, political philosophy.

In the words of political philosopher Leo Strauss, "All political action has then in itself a directedness towards knowledge of the good: of the good life, or the good society."[9] Strauss means here that all political action is conducted according to some opinion or argument regarding the good. For example a conservative argues that lower taxes are good, while a liberal argues that higher taxes to pay for more government services are good. Both liberal and conservative make a claim about what is good in politics. As Strauss argues, political philosophy aims at replacing opinion about the good with knowledge of the good. Opinion is rarely completely wrong, but it is always and necessarily incomplete. Knowledge is aimed at and quite possibly impossible to achieve, except for the gods.

Story-telling is not philosophizing because, as Aristotle notes, it deals more with particulars and philosophy deals more with universal principles. But story-telling shares a similar relationship to action that contemplation does, as described by Strauss. Story-telling with friends completes the events of our days by capturing or illuminating the meaning of those events. In Chapter One we saw Eva Brann's observation: "We save up the events of our days to tell our friends, feeling that until

---

8   Churchill, *The River War*, vol. 1, 31–36.
9   Leo Strauss, *What is Political Philosophy?*, 10.

our affairs have been told they haven't quite happened: Thus do our friends confirm our lives."[10] Without that meaning, the events would not register in the choice-making activity that constitutes our ethical lives.

In addition to completing action, story-telling is participatory, where friends partake as "characters." I not only reveal myself and my history to you, and you not only reveal yourself and your history to me, but together we intertwine those two stories in our shared adventure through life, and together we can look back on that adventure and discern lines of meaning of our common life. This is included in Aristotle's observation that the essential work of friends is "living together and conversing." Thomas Mann explains this intertwining role of storytelling in his novel, *Joseph and His Brothers*, where Joseph explains his shared story to his Egyptian master and friend: "Literature is a great thing. But greater still, to be sure, is when the life one lives is a story—and that we are in a story together, a most excellent one at that, I am more and more convinced with time. You, however, are part of it because I took you into my story."[11] The life of friends *is* a story, and gets expressed *as* a story.

It is for this reason that Hannah Arendt argues that if politics "produces" anything at all (as distinguished from human endeavors like labor and work that produces artifacts), it produces stories:

> The realm of human affairs, strictly speaking, consists of the web of human relationships which exists wherever men live together. The disclosure of the "who" through speech, and the setting of a new beginning through action, always fall into an already existing web where their immediate consequences can be felt. Together they start a new process which eventually emerges as the unique life story of the newcomer, affecting uniquely the life stories of all those with whom he comes into contact. It is because of this already existing web of human relationships, with its innumerable, conflicting wills and intentions, that action almost never achieves its purpose;

10 Eva Brann, *Open Secrets/Inward Prospects: Reflections on World and Soul*, 51.
11 Thomas Mann, *Joseph and His Brothers*, 1233.

but it is also because of this medium, in which action alone is real, that it "produces" stories with or without intention as naturally as fabrication produces tangible things.[12]

Arendt continues by noting rightly that because everybody starts life in the world while the human story has been going on, nobody is an author, but one is instead an "actor and sufferer." Similarly, Eric Voegelin introduces his magnum opus, *Order and History*, with a similar observation: "Man is not a self-contained spectator. He is an actor, playing a part in the drama of being and, through the brute fact of his existence, committed to play it without knowing what it is . . . . The role of existence must be played in uncertainty of its meaning, as an adventure of decision on the edge of freedom and necessity."[13] For Voegelin as for Arendt, story-telling and myth are the appropriate modes of reflecting upon the human condition and of politics because it is participatory. We contribute our stories with others, and embedded within the pre-existing webs of relations that others who have gone before us have established.

The Purpose of Marlborough

With these general considerations regarding story-telling and political friendship, we can turn to Marlborough. Churchill explains his approach in the "Preface" of Volume One:

> In a portrait or impression the human figure is best shown by its true relation to the objects and scenes against which it is thrown, and by which it is defined. I have tried to unroll a riband of English history which stretches along the reigns of Charles II, James II, William and Mary, William III, and Anne. This riband is always of equal width. Through it runs the scarlet thread of John Churchill's life. In this volume we trace that thread often with difficulty and interruption. It slowly broadens until for a goodly lap it covers the entire

12 Hannah Arendt, *The Human Condition*, 183–84.
13 Eric Voegelin, *Israel and Revelation*, 1.

history of our country and frays out extensively into the history of Europe. Then it will narrow again as time and age impose their decrees upon the human thrust. But the riband is meant to continue at its even spread.[14]

Churchill uses two metaphors to describe his biographical method, and both reflect Voegelin's insight that human beings are actors on a stage, committed to play life without knowing what it is. They reflect Churchill's historical view that, "[i]n our human state there is no separation between public deeds and personal psychology, and the story of the one would be incomplete without the other."[15] The first metaphor is the painting whereby the individual is seen "by its true relation" to his circumstances, especially those with whom he interacts, including of course his friends. The face of the individual receives its depth and contour in relation to those circumstances. The human face is embedded within and defined by those relations. If Churchill wanted to use the metaphor of an actor on a stage, he would have said the actor's character receives its definition by the plot within which it acts.[16]

The second metaphor is the riband, a ribbon customarily used for military honours. This metaphor, which also contains Marlborough's "scarlet thread," suggests the plot, the sequence constituted by English history and Marlborough's actions that help create that history. The riband is of course ornamental, to reflect the glory of great deeds, but it is also composed of the weave in which those great deeds by Marlborough show their "true relation" to the other actors of the plot.

Yet Churchill judges the glory of Marlborough's "red scarlet" deficient in a decisive way. For all his military and political skill, he left no memoir nor a history. This means that Marlborough's actions were incomplete. Churchill's biography is an effort to complete Marlborough's actions on his behalf. Indeed, Churchill indicates that his extensive use of Marlborough's letters, especially to Sarah and to Godolphin,

---

14 Churchill, *Marlborough*, vol. 1, 19.
15 Ibid., 722.
16 This is one of the lessons of citizenship in Aristotle's *Poetics*. See *Friendship is the Form of Politics*, Chapter 3.

constitutes an effort to enable Marlborough, to a large extent, to complete his own actions: "I have followed the method used in earlier volumes of always endeavoring to make Marlborough speak whenever possible."[17] Churchill's extensive references to his own correspondence in *The Second World War* achieves a comparable goal. As noted in a previous chapter, Churchill's method of citing his own memos in *The Second World War*, and Marlborough's own letters, enables the reader to sit in the statesman's cockpit of decision-making. The reader faces the same situation and is armed with the same information as the statesman had at the time. Churchill's summary comes only after he finishes describing the action. Writing with these two perspectives—one in the present and one in retrospective—is a time-honoured method of political education, seen also in ancient Greek tragedy according to Aristotle. The first perspective speaks before "answers to all the riddles were known," and the second perspective speaks when they were solved.[18] That both perspectives are the same is seen in Churchill's claim that, "I could not write in better words now."[19]

This dual perspective describes Churchill the writer. The converse is true of Churchill the political actor. During World War Two, Churchill busied himself so much with correspondence and other documents that it led some of his colleagues to complain he was fighting the war simply to write the history. Upon his reappointment to the Admiralty in September 1939, one official complained to Samuel Hoare (Lord Privy Seal): "He is writing his new memoirs."[20] That same month Neville Chamberlain wrote that Churchill:

> continually writes me letters many pages long. As we meet every single day in the War Cabinet this would seem unnecessary, but of course I realize that these letters are for the purpose of quotation in the Book that he will write hereafter. Hitherto I haven't answered them, but the one I got yesterday

17 Churchill, *Marlborough*, vol. 2, 492.
18 Churchill, *The Second World War*, vol. 4, xiii.
19 Ibid.
20 As reported by Rose, *The Literary Churchill*, 277.

was so obviously recording his foresight and embodied warn-
ings so plainly for purpose of future allusion that I thought I
must get something on the record too which would have to
be quoted in the Book.[21]

Indeed, John Colville reports that by December 1940, Churchill had
planned to "write a book about the war, which he had already mapped
out in his mind chapter by chapter."[22] Rose comments: "It was an aston-
ishing example of premature advance planning: at that point actual
events had not quite reached the end of the second volume of his future
six-volume history. But for Churchill, even the Second World War was
a matter of artistic composition."[23] Elsewhere Rose summarizes the connection between political action and art for Churchill: "In fact he made
important policy decisions and composed memoranda with a view toward how they would appear on the page, in the grand story that he spent
his life composing. He was an artist who used politics as his creative
medium, as other writers used paper."[24] However, the paper completed
the creative medium.

Churchill reflects on this relationship between singer of deeds and
performer of those deeds in his biography of Marlborough. There he criticizes his great ancestor for not writing his own memoir. Marlborough
thought Blenheim Palace would be his monument: "He looked to the
great stones rising round him into a noble pile as one answer which
would repeat itself with the generations."[25] He thought his deeds spoke
for themselves.

Despite Marlborough's affability and talkativeness, he seems to have
distrusted words and distrusted the historians whose histories he regarded as little more than courtier flattery. As he wrote to his wife, Sarah:
"I am persuaded that an honest man must be justified by his own actions,
and not by the pen of a writer, though he should be a zealous

21 Robert Self, ed., *The Neville Chamberlain Diary Letters*, vol. 4, 448. See
    Rose, *The Literary Churchill*, 277.
22 Quoted by Rose, *The Literary Churchill*, 277.
23 Ibid.
24 Ibid., xi.
25 Churchill, *Marlborough*, vol. 2, 1036.

friend."[26] Indeed, Churchill seems astonished that Marlborough never bothered to write his memoir: "he seems to have felt sure that the facts would tell the tale."[27]

Instead, Blenheim palace, built of "great stones" instead of mere words, would tell his story:

> As the Pharaohs built their pyramids, so he sought a physical monument which would certainly stand, if only as a ruin, for thousands of years. About his achievements he preserved a complete silence, offering neither explanations nor excuses for any of his deeds. His answer was to be this great house. This mood has characterized dynasts in all ages, and philosophers in none. Remembrance may be preserved to remote posterity by piling great stones on one another, and engraving deep inscriptions upon them. But fame is not so easily captured.[28]

Churchill's reference to a pile of "great stones" reveals his criticism of his great ancestor. It is a remarkable criticism for someone who grew up in that pile of "great stones." One is tempted to judge it impious. Yet one must also recall Churchill always regarded himself an outsider. He famously quipped he was not a pillar of the Church so much as a buttress. This same ambiguous piety of an outsider is on display here in his criticism of his ancestral home as a pile of "great stones."[29] The reason for

---

26 Marlborough to Sarah, quoted in *Marlborough*, vol. 2, 2.87. On Marlborough's affability and talkativeness, see vol. 1, 732. Churchill cites the judgment of the *Observator* pamphlet as basically in agreement with that of Marlborough: "I don't think the Duke of Marlborough will thank any one for being his Praise Trumpeter, that's a post for a pedant and a sycophant," and, "My Lord Duke is one of the best authors this country has possessed. He's the author of conquests and victories" (quoted in *Marlborough*, vol. 2, 188. See also vol. 2, 1036).

27 Churchill, *Marlborough*, vol. 2, 1036.

28 Ibid., 754.

29 A similar instance of ambiguous piety can be found in Churchill's 1947 short story, *The Dream*, in which he portrays the ghost of his father, Ran-

his criticism is that if Marlborough wished his honour to be remembered, he failed to appreciate fully the significance of history, where mere words prove themselves more than mere because they glorify deeds and thereby give them their life. Marlborough's "monument" pales in comparison to Churchill's own "monument," which is how he characterized his memoirs.[30]

Churchill draws a sharp line between Marlborough (and other "dynasts") and "philosophers" who seemingly are not content with noble but silent piles of great stones. His choice of including Marlborough among the "dynasts" is illuminating, for it reduces the stature Churchill had painted for him in his biography. His choice of words suggests a significant shortcoming that Churchill saw in his otherwise great ancestor.

For his part, Churchill, while not a philosopher, seems to cast his lot with the "philosophers" whose monuments are words.[31] For Churchill, "rhetoric (words ordered in speech or on paper) is not a cheap substitute for action but the very soul of action."[32] In a February 1908 speech to the Author's Club, he claimed:

> Words are the only things which last forever. The most durable structures raised in stone by the strength of man, the mightiest monuments of his power, crumble into dust, while the words spoken with fleeting breath, the passing expression of the unstable fancies of his mind, endure not as echoes of

dolph, appearing before him and demanding an account of the twentieth-century since his death. Upon hearing the terrible tale, Randolph reminds Winston he had never expected him to do much with his life. He indicates his surprise at how well Winston understands the events of the age, and indicates he might have made a name for himself if he had entered politics. Winston offers no response and allows the ghost of his father to disappear, ignorant of his son's accomplishments. As someone who spent most of his life seeking his father's recognition, *The Dream* seems to represent Churchill's definitive repudiation of that need. His reference in Marlborough to Blenheim as a pile of "great stones" fits with that sentiment.

30 James Muller, "Churchill the Writer," 38, citing William Deakin, Churchill's literary assistant.

31 See Plato, *Gorgias*, 514a–c.

32 Manfred Weidhorn, *Churchill's Rhetoric and Political Discourse*, xii.

the past, not as mere archaeological curiosities or venerable relics, but with a force and life as new and strong, and sometimes far stronger than when they were first spoken, and leaping across the gulf of three thousand years, they light the world for us today.[33]

Words as monuments are more durable than "structures" that "crumble into dust."

But the monuments of philosophers are not mere words, but a giving of accounts of the way things are, a *logon didonai* as the ancient Greeks said. This is how Churchill understood his writing of moral history, which elsewhere he refers to as "the sum of things." This is not the totality of reality that philosophers seek, but the totality of political wisdom the statesman seeks. As Churchill elsewhere stated, "The longer you look back, the farther you can look forward . . . . This is not a philosophical or political argument—any oculist can tell you it is true."[34]

Close to the time Churchill was writing *Marlborough*, he made much the same point in his essay, "A Second Choice," where he asks whether he would live his life again. His answer is negative because of several factors, including being too weary to "tread again the toilsome and dangerous path."[35] But the deeper reason is that one lifetime is all that is needed to put oneself on display and under judgment. One's life is the canvas upon which we paint our lives, and from which we give an account of ourselves.[36] Churchill concludes his remarks about Blenheim: "His happiness lost much, and his fame gained nothing, by the building of Blenheim. However, Blenheim stands, and Marlborough would probably regard it as having fulfilled its purpose if he returned to earth at this day."[37]

Yet it is only in "this day," the time in which Churchill writes the biography, that Blenheim could have "fulfilled its purpose" because it is

33 Churchill, speech to Author's Club, in *Winston S. Churchill: His Complete Speeches, 1897–1963*, vol. 1, 905. See Rose, *The Literary Churchill*, 104.
34 Bercuson and Holwig, *One Christmas in Washington,* 70, citing Manchester, *Visions of Glory*, 12.
35 Churchill, "A Second Choice," in *Thoughts and Adventures*, 14.
36 See Jaffa, "Can There Be Another Churchill?"
37 Churchill, *Marlborough*, vol. 2, 755.

only in "this day" that Churchill was housed there (and was born there) to conduct research and to write this monumental biography. Indeed, Churchill throughout the biography is at pains to let Marlborough speak for himself, as Churchill had, at Blenheim, access to all of Marlborough's correspondence, especially with his wife Sarah and with Godolphin: "I have followed the method used in earlier volumes of always endeavoring to make Marlborough speak whenever possible."[38] Elsewhere he elaborates:

> In the main Marlborough's defence rests upon his letters to Sarah and Godolphin. It is strange that this man who consciously wrote no word of personal explanation for posterity should in his secret, intimate correspondence, which he expected to be destroyed, or at least took no trouble to preserve, have furnished us with his case in terms far more convincing than anything written for the public eye . . . . I have sedulously endeavoured to reduce them, in the interests of the narrative, but in so many cases they *are* the narrative, and tell the tale far better than any other pen. They plead for Marlborough's virtue, patriotism, and integrity as compulsively as his deeds vindicate his name. Although no scholar, and for all his comical spelling, he wrote a rugged forceful English worthy of the Shakespeare on which his education was mainly founded. He held the whole panorama of Europe in his steady gaze, and presented it in the plainest terms of practical good sense . . . . Everything Marlborough writes to his wife and cherished friends rings true, and proves him the "good Englishman" he aspired to be.[39]

By reproducing Marlborough's correspondence, Churchill allows Marlborough to be his own bard as much as possible, just as Churchill is his own bard in his *The Second World War*. As Frisch observes, "It was with a view to the difference between action and thought (to the timeless char-

---

38 Ibid., 492.
39 Ibid., 20. Emphasis is Churchill's.

acter of thoughts as opposed to actions) that Churchill wanted Marlborough's activity to be made intelligible. He expected Marlborough to cross that line from action to thought."[40] Blenheim is not the true monument to Marlborough and his deeds, but Churchill's biography is the true monument. As Weidhorn notes, the biography, not the pile of rocks, "completes" the action: "The house is symbolic of the dynasty the general was so eager to found, and, though the line passed on through a daughter, Marlborough would seem to have had his dream of family greatness fulfilled in Churchill, his faithful biographer and emulator. In Churchill, the general could recognize his own heroic stature. Yes, Blenheim fulfilled its purpose."[41]

Marlborough's own words, intended for his beloved wife and friends and mediated through Churchill acting as an amanuensis, "*are* the narrative" and thus "complete" his deeds. To the extent Marlborough seemed to believe in the power of words, he seemed only to trust those words communicated to his wife and friends, those best poised to judge his character because his actions, his virtues, and his vices, affected them most of all.

One of the common criticisms of Marlborough during his career was that his victories were the result of good luck instead of his genius.[42] Churchill's biography demolishes that criticism but Churchill implies the same criticism with regard to Marlborough's silent pile of rocks, and even his "narrative" for his wife and friends. Marlborough won his battles with his own arms, but he needed the pen of Churchill to win his political victory. Marlborough's mode of giving of accounts was to leave things to chance. This is odd especially since the desire for esteem, and the desire to stand in the light of truth, was one of Marlborough's overwhelming desires. Many times throughout the biography Churchill notes Marlborough's desire to have a "decisive battle"—ideally with his friend Eugene—that would prove the ultimate test of his character.[43]

40 Morton Frisch, "Winston Churchill, Marlborough: His Life and Times," 191.
41 Weidhorn, *Harmony of Interests*, 107.
42 Churchill, *Marlborough*, vol. 2, 968–69.
43 Ibid., 603. See also 437, 665, 669.

Marlborough, the consummate man of action, sought to display the entirety of his ethos, but despite his many military successes and victories, he never got that opportunity because all his battle efforts involved making compromises with various alliance factions (i.e., the Dutch). As Commander he never had full control of his forces. Never having had the opportunity to wage "decisive battle," Marlborough seemed content to have his "pile of rocks" display his ethos. Churchill's biography fulfills this desire on the part of the consummate man of action to have his ethos put on display, but does so in terms of the "philosophers" who display their ethos in words, and in a meditation on political wisdom. Churchill's biography completes Marlborough's story on Churchill's terms, which fulfill Marlborough's but in a way beyond the range of his vision. In the manner in which he and Roosevelt, and he and Beaverbrook completed each other's sentences as friends often do, the biography is as much an act of friendship as it is an act of piety toward his great ancestor. Even so, it does not produce a "decisive" account of Marlborough because Churchill, who frequently spoke of the "verdict of history," knew full well that history, which never ends, is always open to reinterpretation.[44]

Conclusion

By treating Marlborough not simply as a great commander and statesman, but by treating the "Old Corporal" as instrumental in the foundation of the modern English nation, Churchill's biography is also an English history, the red stripe that runs through the riband constituting the "island story." Churchill's tale of Marlborough's achievements and friendships is a tale of the civic friendship of England, whose story at this stage is "completed" by Churchill the bard, practitioner and theorist of political friendship.

In casting his lot with the "philosophers," the biography also strives to bridge the gap between thought and practice because it is Churchill's greatest statement of his political wisdom, which he sums up in terms of the practice of virtue-friendship: "One rule of conduct alone survives as a guide to men in their wanderings: fidelity to covenants, the honour

---

44 Rose, *The Literary Churchill*, 154–55.

of soldiers, and the hatred of causing human woe."[45] Churchill reads Marlborough as his contemporary and he hints how Marlborough's statecraft and his conduct of a war on the continent will provide the model for what needs to be done with Nazi Germany. In writing the biography, and thus preparing for his own statecraft, Churchill becomes the friend of Marlborough best equipped to judge his character—two oxen treading out the corn—the "complete" addressee of Marlborough's letters that "*are* the narrative." As Alcinous is ultimately the friend to whom Odysseus sings his song, among "banqueters up and down the palace sit in ranks," so too does Churchill find his true friend in political story-telling in Marlborough.

45 Churchill, *Marlborough*, vol. 2, 996.

Chapter Ten
Friendship with the "Old Man"

> He not only makes laws for his people but writes their songs
> as well.[1]

Friendship is at the core of Churchill's practice of and thoughts about statecraft. This book has shown how, in various modes, Churchill viewed friendship both as an important means for carrying out statecraft, as well as its final purpose, both in terms of forging a political friendship with fellow citizens but also an adventure to share with an equally great friend. The appeals to magnanimity and daimonism show how he, contemporaries, and commentators characterized his ambition for greatness, and I have shown how these two categories are compatible with friendship.

We have also seen some of the limits of friendship. In loving his own and the good just a little more, he could be negligent and malevolent toward his enemies. His willingness to fire-bomb German civilian populations and his hostility toward India are examples of this. His defense of empire is also an instance of perhaps an excessive love of one's own. However, his views are more nuanced than critics realize and at least some of this nuance can be attributed to friendship's importance for restraining the logic of empire that points toward one-man, indeed, apolitical despotism.

Friendship is not a cosmopolitan or universal ethic. Nor is it Christian charity. We saw in Chapter Two how Churchill's magnanimity is not restricted to a "pagan" horizon. His ready willingness to forgive owes much to the Christian ethic of Western civilization. Something similar can be said of his sense of friendship and its relationship with Christian charity. For

---

1 Malcolm Cowley, "Mr. Churchill Speaks," 537.

instance, at the conclusion of his "Moses" essay, he describes the Christian God as: "the God not only of Israel, but of all mankind who wished to serve Him; a God not only of justice, but of mercy; a God not only of self-preservation and survival, but of pity, self-sacrifice, and ineffable love."[2]

Churchill says in *The Second World War* and variously in other places that the "Sermon on the Mount is the last word in ethics . . . . Still, it is not on these terms that Ministers assume their responsibilities of guiding states."[3] As we saw in Chapter Two, this statement (and those like it) could possibly be understood as Churchill's choice of honour, the code of Aristotle's magnanimous man, over Christian ethics in statecraft. However, similar views are expressed by Christian theologians and philosophers throughout the ages. For example, Augustine's own "mirror for princes" focuses on the humility a Christian ruler should practice, but nothing in his argument precludes the need for ferocity in defending his realm, or, indeed, his love of honour.[4] In their different ways, Augustine and Churchill acknowledge how the Sermon on the Mount is the condition of morality and not morality itself, and necessitates a life of prudential judgments attempting but always failing to reconcile, in David Walsh's words, the Sermon's "conflict between an impossible demand and its impossible fulfillment."[5]

Churchill wished to defeat and destroy Hitler, not to befriend him nor probably even to forgive him. Even so, he probably also would have agreed with Socrates that it is unjust to harm one's enemy, even if it is Hitler.[6] Indeed, he showed tremendous compassion toward German

2   Churchill, "Moses: The Leader of a People," 311.

3   Churchill, *The Second World War*, vol. 1, 287–88. See also his lecture, "The Flame of Christian Ethics." Colville reports that Churchill told Montgomery that Christ's greatness differed in kind from that of great statesmen: "He said that their greatness was undisputed, but it was of a different kind: Christ's story was unequalled and his death to save sinners unsurpassed" (Colville, *The Churchillians*, 157, and Sandys and Henley, *God and Churchill*, 197).

4   Augustine, *City of God*, V.19. See also David Bobb, "The Humility of True Religion: Augustine's Critique of Roman Civil Religion" and my *Augustine and Politics as Longing in the World*, chapter 5.

5   David Walsh, *Politics of the Person as the Politics of Being*, 56–65. Walsh notes how the ancient philosophers, including Plato and Aristotle, also understood this dilemma in their reflections upon virtue.

civilians after the war. At Potsdam, he wept at seeing the suffering of Berliners and in *The Second World War* he describes how he rallied to defend German populations from encroaching Soviet armies.[7] If World War Two was total war, involving both rulers and civilians, he at least displayed forgiveness and charity to German civilians. One can do these acts out of a sense of honour, the code of Aristotle's magnanimous man, but it is a sense of honour elevated by Christian charity.

Churchill was somewhat distant from Christianity. He famously quipped he was not a pillar of the Church so much as a buttress, which would suggest he was an outsider who supported the Church for the moral benefits to civilization it provides.[8] He was not a regular church-goer and he appears not to have believed in the immortality of the soul.[9]

However, it is easy in these cases to make too much of Churchill's attitude toward doctrinal or theoretical questions because his actions, his statecraft, tell another story. For example, his disregard or distance from religion is contradicted in his frequent prayers for divine intervention in affairs. He displayed remarkable trust in the divine to care for him.[10] His remarkable fortitude and hope amidst the darkest of days defies explanation in terms of his own capacities alone. He famously proclaimed, "Whether you believe or disbelieve, it is a wicked thing to take away Man's hope."[11] His is a lived example of what David Walsh has described as "hope does not disappoint."[12] His practice of hope contradicts any doctrinal grounds for hope he could have understood.

6   Plato, *Republic*, 335b–d. Both understood genuine "harm" involves making one's enemy more evil.

7   Stelzer, *Dinner with Churchill*, 221, and Churchill, *The Second World War*, vol. 6, 580–81.

8   For the reading that Churchill viewed Christianity exclusively for its political consequences, see Emmert, *Winston S. Churchill on Empire*, 28–29.

9   Not all Christians believe in the immortality of the soul because, for them, the Resurrection of the body is what counts for salvation.

10   For details, see Addison, "Destiny, History and Providence: The Religion of Winston Churchill," and my *The Form of Politics: Aristotle and Plato on Friendship*, Chapter 7, for philosophical analysis of this existential trust.

11   Meacham, *Franklin and Winston*, 29, citing Anthony Montague Brown, *Long Sunset*, 204.

12   David Walsh, "Hope Does Not Disappoint."

Indeed, Churchill, in *My Early Life*, makes a point of highlighting the contradiction between doctrine or theory, and practice, especially in religious matters:

> These matters may be puzzling, but they are certainly not important. What is important is the message and the benefits to you of receiving it . . . . The idea that nothing is true except what we comprehend is silly, and that ideas which our minds cannot reconcile are mutually destructive, sillier still . . . . I therefore adopted quite early in life a system of believing whatever I wanted to believe, while at the same time leaving reason to pursue unfettered whatever paths she was capable of treading.[13]

Rose notes that Churchill's capacity to embrace contradictions, real and apparent, "went far beyond religion." Included within this capacity was his "exceptional predilection for compromise. He was confident that seemingly irrepressible conflicts could be resolved: conflicts between the British and the Boers, Irish Catholics and Protestants, Arabs and Jews, a nuclear-armed U.S.A. and U.S.S.R . . . . His mind was extraordinarily supple, capable of jettisoning preconceived notions and collapsing opposites in a manner that we now might call 'deconstructive.'"[14] Indeed, this Hermetic capacity is the mark of his daimonic soul, for better and for worse, capable of profound friendships on many levels.

Churchill's capacity to embrace contradictions and to leave "reason to pursue unfettered whatever paths she was capable of treading" is a sign of remarkable hope in the existential reality in which he traversed. It reflects a profound hope that his actions have support within a moral cosmos that, in perhaps some final sense, ensures good overcomes evil even if our understanding cannot measure up to that reality. It is the hope that sustains the pursuit of justice in this world, and it sustains the possibility for political friendship.

Churchill's existential hope in a moral cosmos that sustains friendship as the form of politics is by no means simple-minded. Neither God

---

13 Churchill, *My Early Life*, 115–17.
14 Rose, *The Literary Churchill*, 31.

nor history guarantees success. Even the writing of history, though establishing one's story and fame more surely than a "pile of rocks," cannot secure them for certain, as the next generation's scholar and scribbler can smash it and thereby render it to oblivion. The ignorance today of Churchill among the schoolchildren of Great Britain is one example of this uncertainty.

The statesman stands on the knife-edge of contingency. In his essay, "A Second Choice," he remarks of the practicing statesman: "Imagination bifurcates and loses itself along the ever-multiplying paths of the labyrinth."[15] He makes a similar statement in *The River War*: "every incident is surrounded by a host of possibilities, any one of which, had it become real, would have changed the whole course of events . . . . In the flickering light of conflict the outlines of solid fact throw on every side the vague shadows of possibility. We live in a world of 'ifs.'"[16] Living in a labyrinth world of "ifs" has its attractions for the risk-loving statesman like Churchill or Marlborough. However, somewhere deep inside his soul he must also judge the risks worthwhile and the labyrinth somehow navigable, which comes from a profound sense of hope that somehow and somewhere those risks will be justified. The statement, "If you're going through hell, keep going," is likely misattributed to Churchill but it captures the core of his existential hope. Even hell cannot demand we abandon all hope.

Churchill also expressed such hope by the divine care he believed stood over him. The most famous example is probably his reflection upon becoming Prime Minister, written in the last paragraph of the first volume of *The Second World War*: "I was conscious of a profound sense of relief. At last I had the authority to give directions over the whole scene. I felt as if I were walking with destiny, and that all my past life had been but a preparation for this hour and for this trial."[17] Other examples of providential care include the prayers he offered up while hiding in a mineshaft to avoid capture by the Boers, and even his exclusion

---

15 Churchill, "A Second Choice," in *Thoughts and Adventures*, 9.
16 Churchill, *The River War*, vol. 1, 235. See Rose, *The Literary Churchill*, 91.
17 Churchill, *The Second World War*, vol. 1, 601.

from office during his "wilderness years," as when Stanley Baldwin made a point he would not include him in government: "There was much mocking in the Press about my exclusion. Now one can see how lucky I was. Over me beat the invisible wings."[18] Churchill claimed on the eve of the Battle of Alamein: "I sometimes have a feeling, in fact I have it very strongly, a feeling of interference. I want to stress that. I have a feeling sometimes that some guiding hand has interfered. I have the feeling that we have a guardian because we have a great cause, and that we shall have that guardian as long as we serve that cause faithfully."[19] Finally, in June 1950, on the eve of the Korean War, as leader of Opposition he told his shadow cabinet: "The old man is very good to me. I could not have managed this [Korean] situation had I been in Attlee's place. I should have been called a warmonger." Asked by Sir David Maxwell – Fyfe who the "old man" was, Churchill replied, "God, Sir Donald."[20]

As Odysseus had his Athena, as Socrates had his daimon, as Moses had God, so too did the daimonic Churchill have his "old man." Having traversed the dark night of the soul, the statesman is grateful for the providential care he has enjoyed by being able to keep going. The statesman with the burning bush inside him is thankful for having received the burning bush. Thus Harry Jaffa states of Churchill and the intelligibility of the life of action in Churchill: "Contemplating life as a whole must give us faith that, in the long run, chance is not merely indifferent to human excellence"[21] God and the gods, it appears, care for statesmen. They are his friends.

Voegelin reports that on the evening of Plato's death at the age of 81, he had a Thracian girl play the flute to him: "The girl could not find the beat of the *nomos*. With a movement of his finger, Plato indicated to her the Measure."[22] Voegelin takes this as a sign of Plato's profoundly

18 Ibid., 162.
19 Addison, "Destiny, History and Providence," 248, citing Churchill's speech to a conference of delegates of coal mine owners and miners on October 31, 1942.
20 Ibid.
21 Harry Jaffa, "Can There Be Another Winston Churchill?"
22 Voegelin, *Plato and Aristotle*, 268.

musical soul. Similarly, Churchill's daughter Sarah reports that when he slipped into his final coma, he remained an artist to the end: "Sometimes his hand would begin to move in painting gestures, and we would know that he was happy. Needless to say, we wondered what particular scene was crossing his mind."[23] Very likely, he was painting the "whole scene" with "perfect comprehensive judgment," "untiring eye and absolute self-lessness," friends and all.

---

23 Sarah Churchill, *Keep on Dancing*, 333–36. See Rose, *The Literary Churchill*, 448.

Bibliography

Works by Winston Churchill

"Are Parliaments Obsolete?" *Pearson's Magazine*, June 1934: 555–56.

"Bolshevism and Imperial Sedition." Speech delivered November 4, 1920. In *Winston S. Churchill: His Complete Speeches*, vol. 3, edited by Robert Rhodes James, 3026. New York: Chelsea House Publishers, 1974.

"Civilisation." Chancellor's Address delivered July 2, 1938 at University of Bristol. In *Winston S. Churchill: His Complete Speeches*, vol. 6, edited by Robert Rhodes James, 5990–91. New York: Chelsea House Publishers, 1974.

Churchill in His Own Words, edited by Richard Langworth. London: Ebury Press, 2012.

The Churchill War Papers. Vols. II–III, edited by Martin Gilbert. New York: W.W. Norton, 2001.

The Dream. Delray Beach, FL: Levenger Press, 2005.

"The Flame of Christian Ethics." Speech Delivered at University of Oslo, May 12, 1948. In *Winston S. Churchill: His Complete Speeches, 1897–1963*, vol. 7, edited by Robert Rhodes James, 7643–35. New York: Chelsea House Publishers, 1974.

Great Contemporaries. Edited by James W. Muller. Wilmington, DE: Intercollegiate Studies Institute, 2009.

A History of the English-Speaking Peoples. 3 volumes. London: Cassell, 1956–58.

Marlborough: His Life and Times. 2 volumes. Chicago: University of Chicago Press, 2002.

My Early Life. New York: Charles Scribner's Sons, 1958.

My Early Life: A Roving Commission. London: Thornton Butterworth Limited, 1930.

The River War. London: Longmans, Green, 1899.

Savrola: A Tale of the Revolution in Laurania. New York: Random House, 1956.

"The Scaffolding of Rhetoric." In *Young Soldier, 1896–1901*. Volume 2 of *The Churchill Documents,* edited by Randolph S. Churchill, 816–21. Hillsdale, MI: Hillsdale College Press, 2006. Online edition: https://winstonchurchill.hillsdale.edu/the-scaffolding-of-rhetoric/

The Second World War. 6 volumes. Edited by John Keegan. New York: Mariner Books, 2003.

"Speech on Rebuilding the House of Commons (1943)." In *Conservatism: An Anthology of Social and Political Thought from David Hume to the Present*, edited by Jerry Z. Muller, 285–59. Princeton: Princeton University Press, 1997.

Thoughts and Adventures. Edited by James W. Muller. Wilmington, DE: Intercollegiate Studies Institute, 2009.

"The Upkeep of the Aristocracy." In *Never Given In! The Best of Winston Churchill's Speeches*, edited by Winston S. Churchill, 37–38. London, Bloomsbury, 2013.

"Whither Britain?" *Listener*. January 17, 1934: 215.

Secondary Works

Addison, Paul. "Destiny, History and Providence: The Religion of Winston Churchill." In *Public and Private Doctrine: Essays in British History Presented to Maurice Cowling*, edited by Michael Bentley, 236–50. Cambridge: Cambridge University Press, 1993.

Aldous, Richard. *Reagan and Thatcher: The Difficult Relationship*. London: Arrow, 2013.

Aquinas, Thomas. *Summa Theologiae*. Translated by the Fathers of the English Dominican Province. 5 vols. Westminster, MD: Christian Classics, 1948.

Arendt, Hannah. *On Revolution*. New York: Penguin Books, 1963.

———. *The Human Condition*. Chicago: University of Chicago Press, 1958.

Aristotle. *The Complete Works of Aristotle*. Edited by Jonathan Barnes. 2 volumes. Princeton: Princeton University Press, 1984.

———. *Nicomachean Ethics*. Translated by J. Sachs. Newburyport, MA: Focus Publishing, 2002.

———. *Poetics*. Translated by Joe Sachs. Newburyport, MA: Focus Publishing, 2006.

———. *Politics*. Translated by Carnes Lord. Chicago: University of Chicago Press, 1984.

Arnn, Larry P. *Churchill's Trial: Winston Churchill and the Salvation of Free Government*. Nashville, TN: Nelson Books 2015.

Augustine. *City of God*. Translated by R. W. Dyson. Cambridge: Cambridge University Press, 1998.

Augustine. *Confessions*. Translated by F. J. Sheed. Indianapolis: Hackett, 2006.

Bagehot, Walter. *Physics and Politics, or thoughts on the application of principles of natural selection and inheritance to political society*. Westmead: Gregg International Publishers, 1971 [1872].

Beaverbrook, Lord (Max Aitken). *Friends: Sixty Years of Intimate Personal Relations with Richard Bedford Bennett*. London: Heinemann, 1959.

———. "Two War Leaders." *History Today*, August 1, 1973: 551–52.

Bercuson, David J. and Holger H. Herwig. *One Christmas in Washington: The Secret Meeting Between Roosevelt and Churchill That Changed the World*. New York: The Overlook Press, 2005.

Bishirjian, Richard J. "Daimonic Men." *Modern Age*, Winter 1996: 159–63.

Black, Conrad. *Franklin Delano Roosevelt: Champion of Freedom*. New York: Public Affairs, 2003.

Bobb, David. "The Humility of True Religion: Augustine's Critique of Roman Civil Religion." In *Civil Religion in Political Thought: Its Perennial Questions and Enduring Relevance in North America*, edited by Ronald Weed and John von Heyking, 66–92. Washington, DC: Catholic University of America Press, 2010.

Brann, Eva. *Open Secrets/Inward Prospects: Reflections on World and Soul*. Philadelphia: Paul Dry Books, 2003.

Brown, Anthony Montague. *Long Sunset*. Ashford: Podkin Press, 2009.

Burke, Edmund. *Reflections on the Revolution in France.* Volume 2 of *Select Works of Edmund Burke,* edited by Francis Canavan. Indianapolis: Liberty Fund, 1999.

Butler, Susan. *Roosevelt and Stalin: Portrait of a Partnership.* New York: Knopf, 2015.

Churchill, Sarah. *Keep on Dancing.* New York: Coward, McCann and Geoghegan, 1981.

Clausewitz, Carl von. *On War,* translated by Michael Howard and Peter Paret. Princeton: Princeton University Press, 1976.

Cohen, Eliot A. "Churchill at War." *Commentary,* 83(5) May 1, 1987: 40–49.

Collins, Ace. *Stories Behind the Hymns That Inspire America.* Grand Rapids, MI: Zondervan, 2003.

Colville, John. *The Churchillians.* London: Weidenfeld and Nicolson, 1981.

———. *Fringes of Power: 10 Downing Street Diaries, 1939–1955.* New York: W.W. Norton, 1985.

———. *Winston Churchill and His Inner Circle.* New York: Simon and Schuster, 1981.

Coombs, David. *Sir Winston Churchill's Life Through His Paintings.* Oxford: Chaucer Press, 2003.

Cooper, Barry. *Alexander Kennedy Isbister: A Respectable Critic of the Honourable Company.* Ottawa: Carleton University Press, 1988.

———. "Aron's Clausewitz." In *Political Reason in the Age of Ideology: Essays in Honor of Raymond Aron,* edited by Daniel J. Mahoney and Bryan-Paul Frost, 75–104. New York: Transaction Books, 2007.

Coote, Colin R. *The Other Club.* London: Sidgwick and Jackson, 1971.

Costigliola, Frank. *Roosevelt's Lost Alliances: How Personal Politics Helped Start the Cold War.* Princeton: Princeton University Press, 2012.

Cowley, Malcolm. "Mr. Churchill Speaks." *New Republic,* April 21, 1941: 537.

Crosson, Frederick. "Structure and Meaning in St. Augustine's *Confessions.*" In *The Augustinian Tradition,* edited by Gareth B. Matthews, 27–38. Berkeley: University of California Press, 1999.

Deutsch, Kenneth L. "Thomas Aquinas on Magnanimous and Prudent Statesmanship." In *Magnanimity and Statesmanship,* edited by Carson Holloway, 49–66. Lanham, MD: Lexington Books, 2008.

Dilks, David. *Churchill and Company: Allies and Rivals in War and Peace.* London: I. B. Tauris, 2012.

Douglas, R. M. *Orderly and Humane: The Expulsion of the Germans After the Second World War.* New Haven, CT: Yale University Press, 2012.

Emmert, Kirk. *Winston S. Churchill on Empire.* Foreword by Harry Jaffa. Durham, NC: Carolina Academic Press, 1989.

Fornieri, Joseph R. "Lincoln and Biblical Magnanimity." In *Magnanimity and Statesmanship*, edited by Carson Holloway, 171–96. Lanham, MD: Lexington Books, 2008.

Freeman, David. "The Friendship Between Churchill and F. E. Smith." *Finest Hour*, vol. 139: 28–35. http://www.winstonchurchill.org/images/finesthour/pdf/Finest_Hour_139.pdf.

Frisch, Morton. "The Intention of Churchill's 'Marlborough.'" *Polity*, vol. 12, no. 4 (Summer 1980): 560–74.

George, Robert Lloyd. *David & Winston: How the Friendship Between Churchill and Lloyd George Changed the Course of History.* London: John Murray, 2006.

Gibbs, Nancy and Michael Duffy. *The Presidents Club: Inside the World's Most Exclusive Fraternity*, New York: Simon and Schuster, 2012.

Gilbert, Martin. *Churchill and America.* New York: Free Press, 2005.

———. *Churchill's Political Philosophy.* London: British Academy, 1981.

———. *Will of the People: Churchill and Parliamentary Democracy.* Toronto: Vintage Canada, 2006.

———. *1922–1939.* Volume 5 of *Winston S. Churchill.* London: Heinemann, 1976.

———. *Road to Victory, 1941–1945.* Volume 7 of *Winston S. Churchill.* London: Heinemann, 1986.

———. *"Never Despair," 1945-1965.* Volume 8 of *Winston S. Churchill.* London: Heinemann, 1988.

Goodwin, Doris Kearns. *No Ordinary Time: Franklin and Eleanor Roosevelt: The Home Front in World War II.* New York: Simon and Schuster, 1994.

Hamilton, Alexander, John Jay, and James Madison. *The Federalist.* Gideon Edition, edited by George W. Carey and James McClellan. Indianapolis: Liberty Fund, 2001.

Harris, Frances. *The General in Winter: The Marlborough-Godolphin Friendship and the Reign of Queen Anne*. Oxford: Oxford University Press, 2017.

Havers, Grant. *Leo Strauss and American Democracy*. DeKalb: Northern Illinois University Press, 2013.

Havardi, Jeremy. *The Greatest Briton: Essays on Winston Churchill's Life and Political Philosophy*. London: Shepheard-Walwyn Publishers Ltd., 2009.

Henningsen, Manfred. "The Dream Worlds of Tyrants." In *Politikos: Vom Element des Persönlichen in der Politik: Festschrift für Tilo Schabert zum 65. Geburtstag*. Edited by Karl-Heinz Nusser, Matthias Riedl, and Theresia Ritter, 131–46. Berlin: Duncker & Humblot, 2008.

Hermiston, Roger. *All Behind You, Winston: Churchill's Great Coalition, 1940–45*. London: Aurum Press, 2016.

Heyking, John von. *Augustine and Politics as Longing in the World*. Columbia, MO: University of Missouri Press, 2001.

———. *The Form of Politics: Aristotle and Plato on Friendship*. Montréal-Kingston: McGill-Queens University Press, 2016.

———. "Friendship as Precondition and Consequence of Creativity in Politics." In *The Primacy of Persons in Politics: Empiricism and Political Philosophy*, edited by John von Heyking and Thomas Heilke, 79–106. Washington, DC: Catholic University Press, 2013.

———. "Liberal Education Embedded in Civic Education for Responsible Government: The Case of John George Bourinot." In *Liberal Education and Canadian Political Culture: The Legacy, The Need, And The Prospects*, edited by David Livingstone, 44–76. Montréal-Kingston: McGill-Queens University Press, 2015.

———. "'The Sum Total of Our Relationships to Others': Kant on Friendship." In *The Luminosity of Modernity: Essays on the Political Thought of David Walsh*, edited by Rouven Steeves and Steven McGuire. Forthcoming.

Hobbes, Thomas. *Leviathan*. Edited by Richard Tuck. Cambridge: Cambridge University Press, 1996.

Hollis, General Sir Leslie. *One Marine's Tale*. London: Andre Deutsch, 1956.

Homer. *The Odyssey*. Translated by Joe Sachs. Philadelphia: Paul Dry, 2015.

Huizinga, Johannes. *Homo Ludens: A Study of the Play Element in Culture.* Boston: Beacon Press, 1971.

Jaffa, Harry. "Aristotle and the Higher Good," *New York Times*, 1 July 2011. http://www.nytimes.com/2011/07/03/books/review/book-review-aristotles-nicomachean-ethics.html?pagewanted=all&_r=0.

———. "Can There Be Another Winston Churchill?" *Claremont Review of Books*, February 2004. https://www.claremont.org/basicPageArticles/can-there-be-another-winston-churchill/.

James, William. *The Varieties of Religious Experience.* New York: Modern Library, 1999.

James, Lawrence. *Churchill and Empire: A Portrait of an Imperialist.* New York: Pegasus Books, 2014.

Jenkins, Roy. *Churchill: A Biography.* New York: Penguin, 2001.

Johnson, Boris. *The Churchill Factor.* London: Hodder and Stoughton, 2014.

Johnson, Paul. "Indispensable Friendship." *Forbes*, vol. 178, Issue 5 (September 18, 2006): 41.

Kant, Immanuel. "Anthropology From a Pragmatic Point of View." In *Anthropology, History, and Education*, edited by Günter Zöller and Robert Louden, 377–82. Cambridge: Cambridge University Press, 2007.

———. "Postscript to Christian Gottlieb Mielcke's Lithuanian-German and German-Lithuanian Dictionary." In *Anthropology, History, and Education*, edited by Günter Zöller and Robert Louden, 432. Cambridge: Cambridge University Press, 2007.

Kinvig, Clifford. *Churchill's Crusade: The British Invasion of Russia, 1918–1920.* London: Hambledon Continuum, 2006.

Klopp, Onno. *Der Fall des Hauses Stuart.* Vol. XII. Vienna: W. Braumüller, 1875–88.

Kass, Leon. *The Hungry Soul: Eating and the Perfecting of Our Nature.* New York: Free Press, 1994.

Keys, Mary. "Humility and Greatness of Soul." *Perspectives on Political Science*, 37(4) (2008): 217–22.

Kotkin, Stephen. Vol. 1 of *Stalin: Paradoxes of Power, 1878–1928.* New York: Penguin, 2014.

Leibovitch, Mark. *This Town: Two Parties and a Funeral in America's Gilded Capital.* New York: Blue Rider Press, 2013.

Lysagt, Charles. "Churchill's Faithful Chela." *History Today*, February 2002: 43–45.

Mahoney, Daniel J. *The Conservative Foundations of the Liberal Order: Defending Democracy Against its Modern Enemies and Immoderate Friends.* Wilmington, DE: Intercollegiate Studies Institute Books, 2010.

Mann, Thomas. *Joseph and His Brothers*. Translated by John E. Woods. New York: Alfred A. Knopf, 2005.

Mansfield, Harvey. *America's Constitutional Soul*. Baltimore: Johns Hopkins University Press, 1991.

———. "Party Government and the Settlement of 1688." *American Political Science Review*, Vol. 58, No. 4 (December 1964): 933–46.

Meacham, Jon. *Franklin and Winston: An Intimate Portrait of an Epic Friendship*. New York: Random House, 2004.

Miller, Stephen. *Conversation: A History of a Declining Art*. New Haven: Yale University Press, 2006.

Montefiore, Simon Sebag. *Stalin: The Court of the Red Tsar*. London: Weidenfeld and Nicolson, 2015.

Morrissey, William. "The Statesman as Great-Souled Man: Winston Churchill." In *Magnanimity and Statesmanship*, edited by Carson Holloway, 197–220. Lanham, MD: Lexington Books, 2008.

Morton, H. V. *Atlantic Meeting*. Toronto: Reginald Saunders, 1943.

Muller, James. "Churchill's Understanding of Politics." In *Educating the Prince: Essays in Honor of Harvey Mansfield*, edited by Mark Blitz and William Kristol. Lanham, MD: Rowman and Littlefield Publishers, 2000.

———. "'A Good Englishman': Politics and War in Churchill's Life of Marlborough." *Political Science Reviewer*, 18(1) (1988): 85–125.

———. "Imperialism as the Highest Stage of Civilization." *Review of Politics*, 53(3) (Summer, 1991): 580–82.

———. "A Lesson That Had Sunk into His Nature: The Dangers of a Subordinate Position." Paper presented to the Annual Meeting of the American Political Science Association, San Francisco, CA, September 2015.

———. "Churchill the Writer." *Wilson Quarterly*, 18(1) (1994): 38–48.

Newell, Waller. *The Soul of a Leader*. New York: Harper, 2009.

———. *Tyranny: A New Interpretation*. Cambridge: Cambridge University Press, 2013.

Oakeshott, Michael. *Rationalism in Politics*. Indianapolis: Liberty Fund, 1991.

Pendar, Kenneth. *Adventure in Diplomacy*. London: Cassell, 1966.

Perkins, Frances. *The Roosevelt I Knew*. New York: Viking Press, 1946.

Plato. *The Laws of Plato*. Translated by T. L. Pangle. Chicago: University of Chicago Press, 1988.

———. *Republic*. Translated by Joe Sachs. Newburyport, MA: Focus Publishing, 2007.

———. *Phaedrus*. Translated by J. H. Nichols, Jr. Ithaca, NY: Cornell University Press, 1998.

Purnell, Sonia. *Clementine: The Life of Mrs. Churchill*. New York: Viking, 2015.

Richard, David Adams. *Lord Beaverbrook*. Toronto: Penguin, 2008.

Roberts, Andrew. *Masters and Commanders: The Military Geniuses Who Led the West to Victory in World War II*. London: Penguin, 2008.

———. "Winston Churchill and Religion—A Comfortable Relationship with the Almighty." *Finest Hour*, vol. 163, Summer 2014. https://www.winstonchurchill.org/publications/finest-hour/finest-hour-163/churchill-proceedings-winston-churchill-and-religion-a-comfortable-relationship-with-the-almighty

———. "The Goat and the Bulldog." *History Today*, October 2009: 72.

———. "The death of Winston Churchill was the day the Empire died." *The Telegraph*, January 18, 2015. http://www.telegraph.co.uk/history/11351639/The-death-of-Winston-Churchill-was-the-day-the-Empire-died.html.

Roosevelt, Franklin Delano. *Complete Presidential Press Conferences of Franklin Delano Roosevelt, 1933–1945*, vol. XXIV, edited by Jonathan Daniels. New York: Da Capo Press, 1973.

———. *The Public Papers And Addresses of Franklin D. Roosevelt*, volume II, edited by Samuel I. Rosenman. New York: Russell and Russell, 1969 [1938–50].

Rose, Jonathan. *The Literary Churchill*. New Haven: Yale University Press, 2014.

Russell, Peter H. *The First Summit and the Atlantic Charter*. Booklet published by the Churchill Society for the Advancement of Parliamentary Democracy and the International Churchill Society – Canada. Undated.

Salkever, Stephen. "Taking Friendship Seriously: Aristotle on the Place(s) of *Philia* in Human Life." In *Friendship and Politics: Essays in Political Thought*, edited by John von Heyking and Richard Avramenko, 53–83. Notre Dame: University of Notre Dame Press, 2008.

Sandys, Jonathan and Wallace Henley. *God and Churchill: How the Great Leader's Sense of Divine Destiny Changed His Troubled World and Offers Hope for Ours*. Carol Stream, IL: Tyndale Momentum, 2015.

Schabert, Tilo. *Boston Politics: The Creativity of Power*. Boston: Walter de Gruyter, 1989.

———. "A Classical Prince: The Style of Francois Mitterrand." In *Philosophy, Literature, and Politics: Essays Honoring Ellis Sandoz*, edited by Charles Embry and Barry Cooper, 234–57. Columbia, MO: University of Missouri Press, 2005.

———. "A Continuing Strife Towards Cosmogony: History," paper presented to Eric Voegelin Society, San Francisco, CA, September 2015.

———. *How World Politics is Made: France and the Reunification of Germany*. Edited by Barry Cooper. Translated by John Tyler Tuttle. Columbia, MO: University of Missouri Press, 2002.

———. "Introduction: The Eranos Experience." In *Pionere, Poeten, Professoren: Eranos und der Monte Verità in der Zivilisationsgeschichte des 20. Jahrhunderts*, edited by Elisabetta Barone, Matthias Riedl, Alexandra Tischel, 9–20. Würzburg: Königshausen und Neumann, 2004.

Schneer, Jonathan. *Ministers at War: Winston Churchill and His War Cabinet*. New York: Basic Books, 2015.

Scott, Jonathan. *When the Waves Ruled Britannia: Geography and Political Identities, 1500–1800*. Cambridge: Cambridge University Press, 2011.

Self, Robert, ed. *The Neville Chamberlain Diary Letters*. Volume 4. Aldershot: Ashgate, 2000–05.

Shell, Susan. "'*Nachschrift eines Freundes*': Kant on Language, Friendship and the Concept of a People." *Kantian Review*, 15(1) March 2010: 88–117.

Smith, F.E. (Lord Birkenhead). *Contemporary Personalities*. London: Cassel, 1924.

Sokolowski, Robert. "The Phenomenology of Friendship." *Review of Metaphysics* 55 (2002): 451–70.

Solzhenitsyn, Alexander. *In the First Circle*, translated by Harry T. Willets. New York: Harper Perennial, 2009.

Stafford, David. *Roosevelt and Churchill: Men of Secrets*. New York: The Overlook Press, 1999.

Stelzer, Cita. *Dinner With Churchill: Policy-Making at the Dinner Table*. Pine Street: Short Books, 2011.

Stern-Gillet, Suzanne. "Souls Great and Small: Aristotle on Self-Knowledge, Friendship, and Civic Engagement." In *Ancient and Medieval Concepts of Friendship*, edited by Suzanne Stern-Gillet and Gary M. Gurtler, 51–83. Albany, NY: SUNY Press, 2014.

Steyn, Richard. *Churchill and Smuts: The Friendship*. Johannesburg: Jonathan Ball Publishers, 2018.

Strauss, Leo. "Churchill's Greatness." *Weekly Standard* 5, no. 3 (January 4, 2000). http://www.weeklystandard.com/Content/Protected/Articles/000/000/010/507glmbp.asp#

———. Letter to Karl Löwith, August 20, 1946, reprinted in the *Independent Journal of Philosophy*, vol. 4 (1983): 111.

———. *On Tyranny*. Revised and Expanded Edition including the Strauss-Kojève Correspondence, edited by Victor Gourevitch and Michael S. Roth. New York: Free Press, 1991.

———. *What is Political Philosophy?* Chicago: University of Chicago Press, 1988 [1959].

Tabachnick, David and Toivo Koivukoski, eds. *Enduring Empire: Ancient Lessons for Global Politics*. Toronto: University of Toronto Press, 2009.

Taylor, A. J. P. *Beaverbrook*. London: Hamilton, 1972.

Telfer, Elizabeth. "Friendship." In *Other Selves: Philosophers on Friendship*, edited by Michael Pakaluk, 250–67. Indianapolis: Hackett, 1991.

Theakston, Kevin. "'Part of the Constitution': Winston S. Churchill and Parliamentary Democracy." *Finest Hour*. Vol. 136. August 2007: 30–36.

———. *Winston Churchill and the British Constitution*. London: Politico's, 2004.

Tocqueville, Alexis de. *Democracy in America*. Translated by Harvey Mansfield and Delba Winthrop. Chicago: University of Chicago Press, 2000.

———. *Writings on Empire and Slavery*, edited by Jennifer Pitts. Baltimore: Johns Hopkins University Press, 2001.

Toye, Richard. *Churchill's Empire: The World That Made Him and the World He Made*. New York: St. Martin's Griffin, 2011.

Voegelin, Eric. *Anamnesis: On the Theory of History and Politics*. Vol. 6 of *Collected Works of Eric Voegelin*. Edited by David Walsh. Translated by M. J. Hanak and Gerhart Niemeyer. Columbia, MO: University of Columbia Press, 2002.

———. *Israel and Revelation*. Vol. 1 of *Order and History*. Baton Rouge: Louisiana State University Press, 1956.

———. *The World of the Polis*. Vol. 2 of *Order and History*. Baton Rouge: Louisiana State University Press, 1956.

———. *Plato and Aristotle*. Vol. 3 of *Order and History*. Baton Rouge: Louisiana State University Press, 1956.

Voltaire. *Histoire de Charles XII*. Vol. XVI of *Œuvres Complètes*. Paris: Garnier, 1878.

Walsh, David. "Hope Does Not Disappoint." In *Hunting and Weaving, Empiricism and Political Philosophy*, edited by Thomas W. Heilke and John von Heyking, 252–71. South Bend, IN: St. Augustine's Press, 2013.

———. *Politics of the Person as the Politics of Being*. Notre Dame, IN: University of Notre Dame Press, 2016.

Weidhorn, Manfred. *Churchill's Rhetoric and Political Discourse*. Lanham, MD: University Press of America, 1987.

———. *A Harmony of Interests: Explorations in the Mind of Sir Winston Churchill*. London: Fairleigh Dickinson University Press, 1992.

Weigel, George. "'A Tiny Bit of a Man': Evelyn Waugh's Anticipation of Donald Trump." *National Review*, March 14, 2016. http://www.nationalreview.com/article/432744/donald-trump-evelyn-waugh-rex-mottram

Weisbrode, Kenneth. *Churchill and the King*. New York: Viking, 2013.

Wheeler-Bennett, John. *Action This Day: Working With Churchill*. New York: St. Martin's Press, 1969.

White, E. B. *Charlotte's Web*. Toronto: Scholastic, Inc., 1952.

Wildavsky, Aaron. *Moses as Political Leader*. Jerusalem: Shalem Press, 2005.

Wrigley, Chris. *Winston Churchill: A Biographical Introduction*. Santa Barbara, CA: ABC-CLIO, 2002.

Young, Kenneth. *Churchill and Beaverbrook: A Study in Friendship in Politics*. New York: James H. Heineman, Inc., 1966.

Index